AMAZON SECRETS

2 BOOKS IN 1:
SELLING WITH AMAZON FBA,
AMAZON FBA.

Table of Contents

Selling with Amazon FBA

Description 7
Introduction 9
Chapter 1 Foundations of FBA 13
Chapter 2 Skills Needed for Amazon FBA 21
Chapter 3 Do Product Ideas Grow from Trees? 27
Chapter 4 Placing Your Order 39
Chapter 5 Set Up Amazon FBA 42
Chapter 6 Branding Your Product & Making It Stand Out 45
Chapter 7 Creating Your Product Listing 50
Chapter 8 What Are the Best Ways to Launch Your Products? 55
Chapter 9 Packing and Setting Up Shipments To Amazon 60
Chapter 10 Amazon FBA and Tax Season 64
Chapter 11 Tools That You Will Need to Get Started 68
Chapter 12 Make Your First $1,000 On FBA 72
Chapter 13 Delays 76
Chapter 14 e-bay Vs. Amazon 79
Chapter 15 How to Use Seller Central To Upload Inventory, Create Shipping Plan, Get Paid, and… 81
Chapter 16 How to Create Bundle To Eliminate Competition ... 85
Chapter 17 Understanding Amazon's Success 89
Chapter 18 Quality Control 93
Chapter 19 Instagram / Facebook Hacks 98
Chapter 20 Is Amazon FBA the Right Service for Me? 105
Chapter 21 Mistakes to Avoid 117
Chapter 22 Frequently Asked Questions 122
Conclusion 129

AMAZON FBA

Description 135
Introduction 137
Chapter 1 How to Find Profitable Products to Sell 141
Chapter 2 Selecting the Right Product to Sell 144
Chapter 3 Ordering Product from Suppliers 151
Chapter 4 Shipping 160
Chapter 5 Creating Your Own Amazon Seller Central Account 169
Chapter 6 Creating Your Brand 176
Chapter 7 Creating Your Product Listing 184
Chapter 8 Selling Fees 190
Chapter 9 Your First Sales 194
Chapter 10 How and Why to Private Label! 207
Chapter 11 Amazon FBA Seller Pricing and Repricing Tools 210
Chapter 12 Driving Traffic to Your Product 222
Chapter 13 How to Get Ungated in Restricted Category? 226
Chapter 14 Scaling your Amazon FBA Business 231
Chapter 15 When to and not to use Amazon FBA? 240
Chapter 16 Tips for Success 251
Conclusion 262

SELLING WITH AMAZON FBA

SELLING WITH AMAZON FBA: LEARN THE BEST STRATEGIES TO BUILD A $10,000/MONTH E-COMMERCE BUSINESS WITH AMAZON. SECRETS OF THE MOST SUCCESSFUL SELLERS ON AMAZON REVEALED.

Description

If you're tired of working a nine-to-five job and are looking for an opportunity to start working for yourself from home, then you have probably looked into the concept of selling on Amazon. While you could sell on Amazon and handle all of your orders personally, taking advantage of Amazon's Fulfillment by Amazon program has many perks and benefits that allow you to grow your business faster and reach higher profit margins than doing it alone.

Of those perks, the most desirable one is that Amazon can handle all of the time-consuming work of packaging and shipping your goods to buyers, along with customer service and handling returns. This allows you more time to focus on finding great products that people will want to buy, and ultimately, more time to do the things you truly love to do.

Of course, for those with money to invest or a product already lined up, the same steps can be applied to create your new income stream on the fast track. For those that want to expand past the introductory method of selling what you already have, we will also discuss the various ways to source new products, expand your inventory, and get the most out of your experience as a seller that utilizes this great service from Amazon.

This guide will focus on the following:

- Set up amazon FBA
- Branding your product & making it stand out
- Creating your product listing
- Amazon FBA and tax season
- Tools that you will need to get started

- How to sell your product?
- Understanding amazon's success
- Quality control
- Mistakes to avoid... AND MORE!!!

Introduction

Amazon is perhaps the most competitive marketplace on the planet. It is a place where more than 2,000,000 merchants fight over 400,000,000 customers. The competition is extremely fierce, considering they have to go against each other and the platform itself. However, there are many resellers who stand as living proof of the success that they have achieved on this channel. Most of them are using a very interesting service provided on this platform called Fulfillment by Amazon. The platform favors the users of this service because of two different reasons. The first one is to make money (obviously). The second one is to help other sellers to have stellar delivery standards. After all, the Amazon shoppers deserve such level of standards when it comes to delivery and customer service. Some of the main perks provided by the FBA option include:

1. Eligibility for free delivery for the Prime members

In plenty of cases, the FBA products are associated with the Prime logo, which sends a strong message to the shopper: the product can be shipped for free within 48 hours, and there are benefits that come with this subscription. Just in the US, there are more than 100,000,000 Prime members; that's why they are known as Amazon's big spenders and loyal shoppers. FBA products are exposed to this group, which offers the FBA merchant a great advantage over the others.

2. Amazon Coupons and Free Shipping

It is apparent that Amazon offers free shipping for products above $25 (regardless if the shopper is a Prime member or not). However, the truth is that most of the FBA products are already in this category. It's also the same when it comes to the Amazon coupons, in which case the FBA goods automatically qualify. They are, by definition, eligible products and, as mentioned in the description of free shipping, this service is applicable for them.

3. Better Rankings

FBA is a criteria that is taken into consideration by Amazon's A9 algorithm. This means that such goods are favored when listing the results, as well as getting better rankings and more sales. Every time Amazon displays results for a search term, the first two pages are the only ones with FBA products. The rest of the pages may not even matter for the average shopper on this platform.

4. Seriously Increased Chances of Getting Buy Box

The Buy Box option is the one that every merchant dream of getting because it promises the best placement on Amazon. This function enables easier sales of a specific product. FBA products have the highest priority in this case.

5. Trusted by Amazon

There is no better certificate for a merchant on the Amazon platform than its seal of approval. It's like a certificate of excellence, a proof that this merchant sells the best quality products and takes special care of their customers.

When it comes to shipping, FBA is the best option if you sell massively on Amazon or it is your main selling channel. The company puts its expertise on the table since the merchant using FBA will benefit from discounted carrier services, as well as professional customer support service related to product tracking, or returns. This is how you can benefit from top-notch services provided by Amazon. However, before rushing in to sign up for FBA, you need to know the costs first because this service doesn't come free of charge. There are fulfillment costs, storage fees (depending on the period your inventory sits in Amazon's warehouse), along with the amount that you need to pay for every sale. Not to mention that, in order to succeed and be at least one step ahead of your competitors, you have to seriously consider advertising as an option to boost rankings and sales (conversions).

Product sourcing is very important when you have to stay competitive, considering finding a supplier that can deliver high-quality and reasonably-priced products is a must. You can get a vague idea of the profit margin when you know the estimated price for which you will sell your products. If you have a merchandise that you know will sell and is not sold by many, you can do the math (estimate all the costs) and decide whether it is worth to go ahead with FBA.

If you decide to embark on the journey to win tons of money by selling on Amazon, then the FBA is definitely the right option to select. However, you can't hope to get high sales if your content is poor. You will need to optimize it, use keywords naturally, structure your product description very well, and include the key features of the product in there. Also, make sure to use high-quality pictures before launching your merchandise. Once you have the first sale, you will already notice that your rank is improving significantly, but you also have to pay attention to reviews to get as many as you can and take them into consideration to improve the quality of your products or provided services. Reviews are the most influential statements for any consumers since they can convert a simple view into sales. Everyone is on Amazon to sell; hence, the more you sell, the better. This should be the main objective for any merchant.

If you take all of the above into consideration, your chances of succeeding will increase significantly. Although this is a very competitive environment, there is no better place to sell products than Amazon. This is the place to be. A large of volume of sales is within your grasp, and it's only up to you to decide how much you want to sell and how visible you want to be to your potential customers. The only thing left to say is: Good luck!

Chapter 1 Foundations of FBA

Fulfillment by Amazon is all about strategizing; the difference between selling as a merchant and selling as a professional with FBA is the amount of time you will have to devote to maximizing your potential profit. Here are some basic guiding principles you will need to be aware of:

Buy Low, Sell High

This is how you earn money as an Amazon seller. There are multiple ways to do this; you can use the stores around you as a local resource for purchasing items cheaply. Depending on where you live, you may even be able to make money off of products that are not available elsewhere, and buyers are willing to pay big money simply for access. You may find yourself buying items at their normal price and selling them for a profit. This will be essential to running your business.

Competition

As an Amazon seller, your competition on the marketplace is huge. You must strive to be the best, most efficient seller you can be; this will lead to better reviews, which leads to higher listings. Amazon is a perfect platform for breeding competition among its vendors. It is set up in such a way to advantage the sellers who are already doing well.

This means to make the most of your business, you will need to run a tight ship, constantly checking to be sure you are offering the most competitive pricing. As you start off, you will need to focus on building credibility among your buyers and improving your reputation so you can move higher up in the ranks. There are strategies you can use to increase your visibility that will be addressed in this guide.

Technology

With Amazon FBA, you will be at your optimal productivity by using technology such as your cellphone to stay current with the top-trending products and to take advantage of the most complex apps on the market to calculate your best chances with selling.

Selling on Amazon FBA requires a level of dedication to working on a computer that those uncomfortable with the idea of adapting to new technology will be wary of. You will need to stay in tune and on top of the latest trends in online marketing if you wish to have a chance against the competition. This guide will direct you to some of the best resources on the market for getting the most out of your business.

What direction will this take you?

There are two ways to sell through Amazon FBA: through retail arbitrage, and with private labeling. People run immensely profitable businesses with both approaches, but they require different commitments.

Each form requires significant investment of time. With proper handling, you can turn your Amazon business into a full-time source of income. It doesn't happen overnight, however, and it takes time to build up the reputation and customer base to turn a sustained and secure source of income. This guide will equip you with the tools to understand the ways of the market, starting with the basics of Fulfillment and moving into the more complex routes, such as private labeling, toward the end.

Create your Account

First things first: you have to have an Amazon Seller account. If you are already selling on Amazon, you just need to register your account and "add FBA to your account." Otherwise, you will need an Amazon Seller Account. Sign up by scrolling to the links at the bottom of the Amazon homepage. Under the Header "Make Money with Us," click on the hyperlink that reads "Sell on Amazon." From there, you can register directly as an FBA seller, or start with your individual seller account.

Depending on what you sell, you may want to start with the individual seller before moving up to a professional seller account. There are advantages to starting with a professional seller account. Professional sellers are able to sell items that are restricted from individual sellers. Professional seller accounts are free for the first Month, after which you can renew your subscription for a fee.

Individual sellers are sellers that ship less than 40 items per month. If you are planning to sell more than that, it is advisable to go for the professional account. There are differences in the fees you are charged as a seller depending on which account you use, which are explained in a later section. You can always upgrade from an individual account to a seller account – however, the opportunity for the first free month of selling professionally is only available when you first sign up. If you know you are serious about Amazon FBA as an investment in your future, go for the professional account and receive the first month free. You could always cancel it before the next month's charges set in.

All you need to sign up is your credit card information, name, address, a professional-sounding and snappy display name, and information to verify your identity.

In order to sell, you must complete a participation agreement that obligates you to fulfill Amazon's terms and conditions for selling. There are guidelines you will need to follow to be eligible to sell and restrictions on what you can and cannot sell. A partial list of guidelines is included in this guide, but be sure to check the Amazon official website for up-to-date information.

Now that you are registered to sell, you must figure out how you will acquire the products you will be shipping. There are many ways to do this, but this book will cover two main methods: arbitrage and private-labeling. Since arbitrage is the main way people usually get started, we will cover that method first for the foundations. Private labeling will be addressed in later sections.

Arbitrage

This is the word used to describe one of the fastest ways to get involved in Amazon FBA. There are multiple forms of arbitrage: be it through retail, garage sales, or online. It is the process of buying items at a discount or on clearance and selling them for a higher price through Amazon

Scanning and Scouting

Scanning and scouting is the most common way to begin your venture in retail arbitrage. Key to retail arbitrage are the apps you will use to scan your products and figure out the likelihood of selling off the items in the store. This business is not about taking chances; there are apps available for calculating the approximate profit you stand to make from selling such an item.

The Amazon Seller app is available for Android and iOS phones. Inventory Lab is another service that some recommend as it offers other tools for increasing your efficiency as well. Other scanning apps, such as Scoutify, Barcode Booty, and Profit Bandit, require a fee but come highly recommended.

In retail arbitrage, you scan the barcode on the product in the clearance aisle of the store. The app will display the information you need to determine how good of a deal it is and how much you are likely to earn selling that item. It calculates the profit for you. Depending on the app, you will also be asked to input the cost associated with your selling of the item – for example, the cost of the shipping materials you will need to send it to Amazon. This cost is one you will need to figure out over a period of time, because it is highly dependent on your personal circumstances.

You can repeat this process with retail items in any store, as well as with products of sale at discounts online and at garage sales. This can be done without an app, but it is easier to use your phone than to write the prices down and checking it at home. In the end, it is a personal preference, and trying both ways to see which is more efficient time-wise will not hurt.

The biggest issue people have with retail arbitrage is the amount of time that one must spend traveling from store to store. It requires a lot of energy. With proper scanning, however, it can pay off. It is generally wise to avoid items that are not less than 50% marked down in price. The best deals are on clearance for over 70% if you can manage it.

This type of arbitrage can be applied at yard sales or discount retailers, particularly with items like books. You will not necessarily be "scanning" if you look up pricing on items online, but the principle remains the same.

Scanning for the First Time

One way to feel comfortable and test out your Amazon FBA account is to scan products around your household that have not yet been removed from the packaging. This will give you an idea of how the apps work so you will be more comfortable when you are in an actual store scanning products. Furthermore, you can capitalize on the profitable opportunities you have lying around at home! Take a trip into the basement and make use of all those unwanted Christmas gifts. You may even go so far as to offer to help cleaning out your relatives' closets. You will be surprised at the rankings some products reach!

It is important to be aware of the restrictions on selling some products. Products with restrictions on them will be labeled as such on the scanning apps, but it is worth digging around the guidelines established by Amazon to know what you are getting into. A later section of this book addresses the very basics of what can and cannot be sold through Amazon, but for this type of information, it is best to go to the source.

With Amazon Doing All the Work, What *Does* the Seller Do?

With Amazon doing all the heavy lifting, what do you do as the seller? Procure the goods and find your suppliers for one thing, which is possibly the most important part of the job. Without the right products and a reliable supplier, there will be no business, to begin with. You have other tasks as a seller (which Amazon will not do for you), include:

- *Keeping Track of Your Inventory* - Managing your inventory is going to be your responsibility. Amazon will notify you when your inventory is running low. It is your job to make sure that the items you sell are always in stock.

- *Marketing Your Products* - Amazon does all the backend work for you so you can focus on the more interesting aspects of the business. Like marketing and promoting your products. Competition is high in the online retail space and you need to put your product in the spotlight and make it visible to people who want your products. Starting a store alone is not going to be enough to drive sales that are going to require some effort on your part.

- *Pay Amazon* - Excellent service comes at a price of course. You will have to pay Amazon the necessary fees for using its storage and fulfillment facilities. However, given the kind of service you can expect from Amazon, fees are well worth it.

With Amazon doing all the time-consuming work for you on your behalf (including storage, order fulfillment, handling the delivery and returns and dealing with the customer service side of your business), the fees you're paying for is essentially for the stellar customer service, which is available around the clock and for reliable shipping and access to the most advanced and largest fulfilment networks in this world.

When it comes to reputation, reliability and top-notch service, Amazon is at the top of its game. Not many e-Commerce retailers are able to match entirely what this giant can do (it is the best in the business for a reason). This contributes to a big part of its success and if you are willing to pay the reasonable fees required, you can be a part of that success too.

Chapter 2 Skills Needed for Amazon FBA

At this point, your Amazon Seller Central account is launched and you are serious about starting your business. You have made the commitment, and you are ready to get started so that you can start seeing profits come through on the commitment that you have made. Before we really get started, however, I want to get clear on some skills that you are going to need, in order to launch your Amazon FBA and make a passive income through your efforts.

Every single business requires a unique skill set that is going to help you earn an income with that business, and Amazon FBA is no different. Although this platform does not require nearly as many skills for you to succeed, it does require you to have some degree of skills so you should be prepared to understand what these skills are, and continually invest in them in order to generate success.

Building Your Competitive Edge

Although building your competitive edge is a strategy, it can also be considered a skill, as you do grow better at identifying, building, and honing your competitive edge over time. Some people seem to have the strength right off the bat and can identify what helps them stay competitive against the rest of the crowd, and then leverage that competitive edge to succeed right from day one. This is often the case when you identify stories of people who started making tens of thousands, hundreds of thousands, or even millions within their first year of business.

Even if you are not particularly knowledgeable or skilled in this area at first, you can certainly build your skill at being a competitive business owner. The key to identifying and growing your competitive edge knows what makes you more desirable over any other business in your niche. For example, Lulu Lemon is an athletic clothing company based out of Vancouver, British Columbia and it uses its competitive edge of being a local company with high-quality clothes to market to its customers. Apple is a well-known technology company that has the competitive edge of having products that are sleek and that have a modern or futuristic design to them, which they use to appeal to their customers with. Every company that has ever generated any level of success has identified its competitive edge, and then made virtually every single decision in their company based on how they can leverage their competitive edge to maximize their success.

When it comes to being a more competitive business owner as a skill, you will find that the more that you think with the mindset of "what is my competitive edge and how can I leverage it?", the more it comes naturally for you to find these competitive opportunities. As a result, it will become easier for you to create that competitive edge even further and leverage it even more for your business.

Branding Your Business

Much like with finding and leveraging your competitive edge, branding your business is both a strategy and a skill that you have to develop over time. On the issue of seeing your brand as a skill, the easiest way to understand why it is a skill is to recognize that your brand is an identity with its own personality. Even if your brand is based on you, it is going to have its own image, tone of voice, and other elements of it that are based on its own personality rather than yours.

To help you build your skill in branding, you can spend as much time as possible getting to know your brand and to understand what it looks like and who it is. Get to know your brand as if you were getting to know a new friend, and put just as much effort into understanding everything from the more obvious surface-level elements of your brand to the deeper and more meaningful elements of your brand. For example, you might already have a decent comprehension of the fact that your brand is represented by yellow and teal and that you use Arial font types with it, and you might know that it has a more playful and fun tone of voice to it. However, do you know exactly what words your brand would use to speak with your audience in order to share a relatable and impactful message with them? Do you know how and where your brand would incorporate yellow and teal into its imagery to create an image that is not only identifiable but also enjoyable to look at? Do you know how your brand would communicate with customers in private messages to create a professional conversation that still held the tone of your brand?

Knowing these nuances helps you really understand the brand that you are portraying and how you can leverage it to connect with other people. It might take time for you to get to know your brand on this level, but eventually, you will find that the image captions or product descriptions that once took you hours to come up with, eventually only take a few minutes. This is because you can effectively "get into character" as your brand and portray your brand in the best way possible, while still leveraging it to earn sales from your customers.

Tracking and Monitoring Analytics

Your analytics are an important asset to your business as they directly tell you what your customers think about the way that you are doing business. For the most part, your customers are probably not going to go out of their way to message you with feedback on how they feel about your new products, or what they think about your latest marketing techniques, which is why analytics matter. Analytics give you the opportunity to identify what marketing materials are working, which products are the most popular, and what is ultimately causing your customers to purchase from you, or not purchase from you if you are seeing a rut in your sales.

When considering analytics, you are going to need to know how to monitor your analytics directly on Amazon FBA, as they are directly linked to your shoppers and visitors. However, you are also going to want to apply the same skills to your social media marketing strategies, in order to see how your marketing strategies are developing, too. This way, you can feel confident that both your marketing efforts and your shop are performing to the best of their ability, giving you the best chances at earning a sale in your business.

Expense Tracking and Monitoring

In addition to monitoring and tracking your analytics, you also want to monitor and track your expenses related to your business. When you first launch a business, it can be easy to get lost in all of the various purchases that you make to get your business off the ground and get it in front of your audience. From your Amazon Seller Central account fees to advertising fees and product-related fees, your expenses can rack up quickly, and if you are not careful, they can take a toll on your business.

Naturally, when you first launch a business you are going to go into the negatives for a while, as you are going to be spending your own cash on these early purchases. At that point, you will not have any sales, so you will not have made enough profits to make up for the money that you are spending on launching your business. For that reason, you want to be modest in the way that you spend money early on, so that you can quickly earn some revenue and pay back the expenses that you put into launching your business. The sooner that you can break even, the better, as this means you are not out on your own expenses to launch your business.

Just because you want to be modest with your expenses, however, does not mean that you want to be cheap in the way that you are spending your expenses. The idea instead is to consider what expenses are necessary and then purchase the best quality of each product or service that you can reasonably afford. This way, you have a great brand to launch with and you can always upgrade or add more expenses or features later.

After you have launched your business, you are still going to need to pay attention to your expenses and track them effectively. You need to make sure that you are always working toward staying profitable and that you are never spending more than you have or more than you have to, in order to operate your business. Keep your expenses as low as you reasonably can, while still running a quality business, so that you are able to run a great business while also earning an excellent profit.

Investing in Your Marketing Skills

When it comes to Amazon FBA, aside from sourcing and purchasing product and then having them shipped to

Amazon, your only other role is to market. With the right marketing skills in place, you can drive huge amounts of traffic to your website and get your products seen. This way, you have higher chances of actually having people purchase your products, which is exactly how you earn your revenue in your business.

As you continue to run your business, you should also continue to work on learning how to grow your marketing skills. Do not be afraid to invest in marketing courses, to take seminars or other learning sessions that can help you learn, and to read about the latest in marketing strategies online. The more that you can keep yourself up to date with how to market, as well as the latest trends in marketing, the more you are going to be able to launch your business with great success.

Eventually, the more successful you grow with marketing the easier it will be for you to get your products in front of customers. This way, you will have an even easier time selling your products because you will be doing and saying all of the right things to get the attention of your audience and to encourage them to look at your shop and possibly purchase your products. Again, the better you get with this, the easier it will be for you to do and the more fluidly you will find yourself earning greater momentum off of each post you make or product you launch.

Chapter 3 Do Product Ideas Grow from Trees?

The building block and foundation of this business that everything else will rest upon is the product(s) and *ultimately* the niche you decide to enter into. Pick the correct one and you've got a niche that can provide a sustainable and steady income for a long time to come; choose a bad one and you're going to be paying Amazon so you can rent space in their warehouse. What we are referring to as niche in this case is the market or industry you decide to enter into, generally you will want to start from a narrow point then expand out. So instead of workout gear, you target a certain niche within that wide market such as yoga gear, running gear, gym gear, or whatever other sub-niche there is inside of workout gear.

Selling products on Amazon follows the same rules as any product that is to be sold to the general public: you need to have demand; you need to target a specific market or customer (not just selling boots, but perhaps more specifically Texas leather boots); and you need a product that can easily be found that stands out from competitors.

Before we get into all of the above though, let's figure out what the heck you're actually going to sell. Well, it's best for you to sell what you want to sell, so what is it that you would like to sell?

Haha, we're not going to leave you in the headlights like that! In descending order of easiest to most 'difficult' ways to finding what product or niche to sell in, this is what we recommend you do:

1. Figure out what your interests, hobbies, and passions are and write down a list of them. Now figure out what items are used or related to these interests, hobbies, or passions. Anything you have great interest or really like doing is a great place to start. Think about the things you do when you procrastinate or the things you daydream or think about a lot.
2. Write a touch list for the next 24 hours. Anything you physically touch or interact with over the next 24 hours; make a long list of all of these items either on paper or on your phone. You can also ask friends or family to do this for you too and to pass the list on to you.
3. Look through your bank and credit card statements and make a list of things you've bought that you could potentially sell. It also helps to consider any products or areas you've found yourself or others frustrated with in terms lack of choice, functionality, pricing or otherwise as there is the potential to fill that void in the market for that product.
4. When watching TV you can get ideas from shows, shopping channels, or late night infomercials. Another good way to get ideas is to sign up to blogs, online magazines or newsletters (email or physical) in certain industries and scour through them when they send you their latest editions.
5. Visit online stores and drill through their categories: Amazon, eBay, Pinterest, Etsy, Alibaba, DH-Gate, Ali-Express, Global-Sources are a few to start with. Make a list of products that you would be interested in selling. Make sure to look at similar or frequently bought items if the websites provide suggestions and also check out the Best Seller lists as they prove the

product is already in demand (be careful here as the demand in certain categories can be so low that a product selling 30 products a month could still be tagged as a best seller)

6. Hit up Google and type in the search field the following (with the quotation marks in the same spot): "Amazon Best Sellers Rank: #number in category" site:amazon.com. So for #number you would put #500 or whatever best seller rank you are targeting and in the category put the name of any category or subcategory you're interested in selling in (i.e. "Amazon Best Sellers Rank: #540 in Sports & Outdoors" site:amazon.com. This will show you the product that is currently ranked at the best seller rank you input in Google on Amazon for the category you selected (generally the product will have changed ranks as Google is slightly delayed), and from there you can visit the product page and see what the product is. You can also check out the items that are frequently bought or similar to the product, or if the product/niche isn't to your fancy, go back to Google and keep changing the best seller rank or categories to get new product ideas.

7. (Advanced) Visit product fairs such as HKTDC, Global-Sources, or Canton Fair and see the products and get to know the suppliers on a face-to-face basis. This is a bit more of an advanced option as it helps to know what type of products to look out for and have the ability to quickly check the viability of certain products whilst you're at the fairs. How-ever if you live closely to where any of these Fairs are held (Hong Kong and China mainly) or you're simply passing by when they're on, there's nothing holding you back

from checking it out! You'll be guaranteed to have hundreds of product ideas swarming in your head afterwards.

To elaborate a little further on option 1 above. What are things you enjoy doing, or what are things you find yourself doing on a regular basis? For all of these activities consider any items that you use, bring along with you, or that are remotely related to these activities or events. It helps a ton further down the track if you can pick a product or niche from this option, especially when you start looking at building a brand around the product or niche.

Why is this the case? Because you know the target market on an intimate level, how is that? Because you are that target market, you are an "avatar" (ideal customer) for the market as long as you can find a product to private label that you would WANT to personally buy, then you can easily market the product and create a brand around it. It will also be easier for you to differentiate the product so that it stands out from competitor's products but more on that later. By taking this option you can leverage what you already know and have experience in and this saves you time and resources later down the track. Marketing efforts will be halved because you don't have to think about what would trigger your customers to buy your products over competitors, you already know what will accomplish that.

Stop - It's Hammer TIME!

Hold off from the above for a second! This is the only time you'll ever hear that around here so we suggest you embrace it. You can save a ton of time if you have a basic understanding of what type of products and niches you should be looking out for to begin with.

Firstly as we've already specified, you will want to look at picking a product you can build a brand around. What's the difference between a product and a brand? Well a product is one passive income stream, a brand represents a business. A brand in this case is Nike, UnderArmour, McDonalds, Coca Cola, and so forth. Okay so how do we build and make a brand? Well you create your own logo (hence private label) with your brand name and work towards selling more than one product in the future. This includes variations to your product. What we mean here is that if you sell stools, there can be many products and variations to a stool, there can be a sitting or standing stool, high or low stool etc, all of these are different products yet are only slightly different. Why build a brand instead of just selling a lot of products individually? Simply put, it's much more sustainable over the long term and arguably results in more profit for the effort and time put in by you. You will want to build a brand that stands out in your market and niche so when people think of you, they think of your products. So if we're trying to dominate the stool market and our brand name is "Three Stoolers" (homage to the three stooges) and there are 5, 10, or more products under this brand, prospective customers can see this and may associate a sense of credibility to products sold under this brand as having more than one product shows that this brand or company has experience selling stools.

The benefits of building a brand far outweigh the costs in terms of resource, time, and effort. As you build a brand you are products are perceived as being more trustworthy and reputable, you will be able to start selling on your own without the help of Amazon (so you begin to run the show the whole way from receiving customers to getting them the end product), you can dominate a niche or market thorough this means capturing more sales and so forth. Eventually you will want to venture into building a blog or website, setting up social media channels however that is a long way away. It's good to keep this in mind though and it's why we have stressed it's a lot easier and smarter to pick a niche or product that you have a passion or interest in, especially when you'll be spending time in this niche 5 or 10 years in the future. As mentioned before however, you don't need to pick a niche that you have a genuine interest in, it only means you'll need to dedicate time and effort towards learning about your target market and the products you're selling or perhaps outsourcing this and paying others to do the legwork for you such as writing content for your blog, website, and social media.

The Winning Factors

Before forming your list of product and niche ideas, keep these factors at the forefront of your mind and it will help you cull down on your initial product idea list. If you'd prefer to just note everything down then cut the list down later that's perfectly fine. Please keep in mind that these are merely guidelines to follow and don't need to be adhered to 100%! If the product satisfies the majority of the factors but misses a few here and there but is still profitable it would be silly not to go for it. You can always estimate the shipping fees or revenue based on the dimensions of your product and units sold per month, it's also possible to have a quick glance at what the cost per unit will be for the product from potential suppliers by checking Alibaba, or Global-Sources. Also if you keep in mind that other sellers will also be following a similar criteria for picking a product, this limits many sellers to the same pool of products and thus stepping outside of this pool can result in less competition and untapped profits. It pays a lot in this business to not follow the crowd and go where the path is less travelled. For now though it's highly recommended you stick to the factors below as best you can for your first product so you can get the ball rolling and gain some experience before you even consider taking any risks. So without further ado, the factors to consider are listed below.

Physical Characteristic Factors

1. Is the product small?

A product less than 18 inches in length (on the longest side) is considered standard sized and anything greater than this will be classed as an oversized product on Amazon. Oversized products result in greater shipping, handling, and storage fees which in turn mean a lower profit margin. Other factors to satisfy a standard sized product are 14 inches or less on the median side and 8 inches or less on the shortest side with the product not weighing more than 20 pounds (roughly 9 kgs). Once a product is classed as oversized you can only store 500 units in Amazon's warehouses to begin with however this can be increased over time if your products are selling. A quick and easy test for this factor is to ask yourself if the product will fit inside of a shoebox, it's generally fine if it's slightly larger than one too.

2. Is the product lightweight?

It's best to go with a product that is as light as possible, anything less than 5 pounds (2.25kg) would be most ideal. The lighter the better for the most part as it simply means lower shipping costs and fees. When it comes to shipping it comes down to weight and volume so it's better to satisfy small and lightweight as opposed to large and lightweight or small and heavy. You can get a rough estimate for what a product will weigh by looking at similar products on Amazon as they will have their weight listed, or you can check the weight of products based off what manufacturers' state on sourcing websites. You will want to clarify the weight of the product directly with manufacturers before engaging with them

      3. Is the product simple?

When you're starting out it's advised to avoid electronics as they have a higher risk of failing and more complexity when sourcing products from manufacturers. Apart from this you'll want to aim for products that don't have parts that break easily during shipping and handling such as glass. Having a lot of moving mechanical parts on a product can also be a risk as there's the potential for these parts to break off. From a long term perspective if any of these three issues ever occurred for a product it would not be a pretty sight as your listing would more than likely have a lot of returns coming back as well as negative reviews, and if you offer warranty you can bet a lot of claims would be coming in. The last thing to consider in this scenario is how dangerous the product could potentially be, say for example with hoverboards that caught on fire in recent times, or knives just because of the nature of them. Try to avoid anything that could result in a potential law suit.

    4. *Can the product be private labeled and modified or improved?* We want to choose products that can be private labeled and by this we mean manufacturers actually manufacture the product and also to ensure you aren't competing against major name brands on a product. For example, Huggies are known for diapers, you wouldn't

necessarily want to compete against them as they dominate such a big share of the market. So it's best to avoid products that have one or two well-known major brands that dominate the market.

By modified or improved we're referring to a product that has the potential to be differentiated from competition in the market in some manner by making slight alterations to the product during the manufacturing phase. This could be something as simple as changing a screwing feature on a product to flip open instead. You can easily find these points of differentiations when researching competitors by looking at their reviews 3 stars and below. Avoid the "me too" products, there's not much point going into a market and offering the same exact product as 5 other competitors as it only makes it harder to stand out. Sometimes you can't help it and you have to go for the "me too" product but if you do, make sure your product stands out in some other way (photos, bullet/description, title, etc.) Go for a product you can differentiate or improve on as it will be better for your brand in the long term and it'll make it easier for you to market and sell your product.

One common way of differentiating a product is through bundling, either selling the product in pairs, threes, fours, or fives, or bundling the product with another related product such as a yoga mat and yoga towel.

5. Can you build a brand around the product/niche and also sell more related products around it?

Hopefully this has been hammered into you enough by now but we're here to build a brand which is a business, not simply sell one product and retire on the beaches of Cabo as that's difficult to do. What we mean by this is that you should do some quick preliminary research on similar items and check how well they are selling. There are a few methods for this such as using Google Keyword Planner or just looking at frequently bought together or similar items on competitor's product pages. An example of this is dog nail clippers and dog hair trimmers, they're related and they can be leveraged for you to cross-promote the products between your customers when you release your second product under the brand. Furthermore you can branch out to other pet items under the brand by selling similar products for birds and cats. A quick trick to helping you identify similar products you can sell is just going on to Amazon and finding sellers who sell the product you intend to, click to their Seller Store page (click on their seller name on the product page) and you can see all the products that they are selling and get an idea of what's possible.

6. *(OPTIONAL FACTOR) Is the product a little weird, odd, or unsexy?*
7. No one really wants to sell unique and weird items. A good test to see if a product satisfies this factor is considering how your friends, family, or colleagues would respond if you told them you wanted to sell this product. If they think it's cool or a great idea than it's possible other people have already thought of it or will think of it in the future and hence there's likely to be more competition. If they will think of you oddly or weirdly, jackpot! This is an optional factor to consider because we'll be looking at assessing our competition anyway during our research phase however it's more likely than not this factor will result in less competition in the future. In this business, you will want to steer away from where everyone else

is going into and be the first to find new land so you have first mover's advantage.

Market Research Factors

These factors deal more with the market rather than the product itself. This research will be primarily conducted on Amazon.

7. Is there enough demand in the market to sell at least 10 units a day?

To determine this you will be using the Best Seller Rank on Amazon for products as a guide. Keep in mind we will want to have a good amount of units being sold in a month for the product, we generally refer to this as the depth of the market. More on this later.

For now we'll do a quick primer as to how the Best Seller Rank works on Amazon. For each major category such as Home & Kitchen, Sports & Outdoors, Toys & Games and so on, they have ALL of the items under the category that are listed on Amazon assigned a best seller rank within that category. How this best seller rank is determined is based on how many sales the product has made and this is updated hourly. So each product under the major category is ranked in the order based on how many sales they have made, so the product with rank of #546 has sold more units than #547 in the category of Home & Kitchen or whatever major category they are in. For this reason, the sales rank number for each category indicates a different number of estimated units sold because the total number of products that are bought in Sports & Outdoors could be less than the total products bought in Home & Kitchen.

8. What price range will the product sell for and will you be able to make $10 profit on each product sold?

If you can sell 10 units a day and earn $10 profit on each unit you'll make at least $3000 profit a month on the product. To estimate what the price range for a product would be just ask yourself how much you'd be willing to pay for it or visit Amazon and see what price the product is being sold for. Look for products in the price range of $15 to $50, anything lower than $15 and shipping fees are more than likely to eat the majority of the profits unless it is a really lightweight and small product. $50 has been set as the upper limit because this is roughly the upper end of where impulse purchase are made. Above $50 and people are a bit more reluctant to buying a product straight off the bat without doing some research into alternative options or the reputation of the company selling the product.

9. How tough is the competition?

How many reviews do your competitors have? Is the market dominated by thousands of reviews and big name brands in the top six spots? How well optimized are your competitor's product listings?

Chapter 4 Placing Your Order

In this section I will be covering how your make the first order for your products with your chosen supplier. You will need to setup an account to begin the ordering process - here are the factors to consider:

Forms: As part of the ordering process, you will generally need to fill in some basic forms. Some suppliers may want to see a reseller's license but this is pretty rare.

Payment Method: You will typically need to make a payment up front, however many suppliers will allow a small down payment if requested. I usually pay a down payment of 1/3, and then complete the final 2/3 of payment before shipment. You will also need to figure out the payment methods that they accept: Wire, PayPal, credit/debit card. I usually use Western Union but there are fees associated with this.

Getting design plans: Some suppliers can do your designs for you, but you can send over files that your designers have created. Find out the specifications for what they require, e.g. file types, image sizes etc.

Making your down payment: Most reputable suppliers will accept a down payment which is a percentage of the total cost. If they do not, I would be skeptical about their legitimacy. You can then pay the remaining payment once your products have been manufactured. I recommend getting pictures continuously to make sure your products are actually being manufactured and shipped out.

Waiting for your product to be made: Whilst you are waiting for your products to be made, you should start making your

Amazon product listing page which is covered in the following sections of the book.

Giving your supplier your FBA information: Before your manufacture ships out your products, they will need to include am Amazon packing and label slip which allows them to be correctly sent to an Amazon fulfillment center. Amazon provides these and you can simply email these to your supplier.

Detailed Shipping Details
FBA Labeling: When your products are in the Amazon warehouse, they will require a 'FNSKU' label. You can get your supplier to do this, but for ease and efficiency I strongly recommend letting Amazon do this for you for a cost of $0.20 per unit.

If you have any issues with labeling, don't hesitate to contact Amazon Seller Support. In my experience, they have been excellent and very thorough with guiding me through the labeling process. They will even stay on the phone and walk you through the required steps.

Having your products inspected: It is usually a good idea to have your products inspected when making your first order. These can be done by a 3rd party, but I recommend having the products sent directly to you so you can inspect the quality of the products and then have these forwarded to the Amazon fulfillment center. This will ensure you don't sell any products that have significant issues which will hugely impact your brand and chances of doing well on Amazon.

Action Checklist
Below is a checklist of actions from the last few sections that you must complete before moving on to the next steps:

- Create a list of 5 suppliers for your top 5 preferred products
- Contact each supplier and ask the questions as previously covered.
- Select the final product to go for.
- Order at least 2 samples for this product from different suppliers.
- Narrow down and choose your main supplier.
- Place your order with the supplier and make your initial down payment.
- Obtain relevant shipping labels from Amazon and send these to your supplier.
- Make the final payment and have your products shipped!

Chapter 5 Set Up Amazon FBA

The first step, as you know, is to set up an account with Amazon FBA. Creating your account is the first step because this is where you are going to gain access to everything that you need to launch your Amazon FBA business. With your Amazon account in place, you will have the main hub for your Amazon FBA business fixed in place, so that you are ready to begin selling on Amazon.

What You Need to Know About Amazon Seller Central Account

Your Amazon Seller Central account is the foundation for everything that you do in your business, as you cannot do anything without this account. Although you could complete this step later on after you have already built the rest of your business out, it might not be a great idea, as this will prevent you from acquainting yourself with the platform and learning to navigate it beforehand. Building your account in advance gives you the opportunity to understand none of the features available to you ahead of time, so when considering the time to launch you is attempting to understand a new platform, in addition to managing a launch. As well, many people find that creating the actual account makes their business feel a lot more real, and helps them stay committed to seeing their decision to launch an Amazon FBA business through in a timely fashion.

Amazon Seller Central is going to give you access to everything that you need to know about your Amazon FBA business. Here, you are going to be able to introduce and design your storefront, manage product listings, oversee customer service inquiries, manage your revenue, and gain access to important information such as when stock needs to be reordered and where to send it to. In your account, you will find options to reorder stock and register that stock with Amazon so that they can actually receive your inventory, which is crucial.

Essentially, everything that you will ever need to do regarding the creation, maintenance, or running of your business is going to involve the Amazon Seller Central account in one way or another. The more you can grow comfortable with the platform now, in advance, the easier it is going to be for you to rely on this platform and use it to run your business.

Creating Your Amazon FBA Account

Creating an Amazon FBA account is simple, and does not take more than a few minutes. You will start by going to Amazon's website and scrolling down to the very bottom of the page so that you can see their footer navigation bar. There, you will see a heading that says "Make Money with Us" followed by a link that says, "Sell on Amazon." Click on that link and it will walk you through the systematic process of launching your Amazon Seller Central account.

Right away, you are going to be offered the decision to make an individual account or a professional account. You will notice that the individual account is free, while the professional account is $39.99 per month. Because you are just starting, it may seem tempting to launch a free account, but note that features such as Amazon FBA are not offered to individual account holders, as these accounts are geared more toward selling your own belongings in a "garage sale" type of business. If you want to run a real retail business through Amazon, you need to have a professional account, so you will need to pay the $39.99 fee to launch your account.

After you start your professional account, you will be required to provide information such as who you are, what login credentials you want to use, and what business you are associated with. You may also need to input important information linked to payment and taxes, which will allow Amazon to pay you your profits and offer you a tax slip come tax season. Make sure that you fill out all of this information now, in advance, so that it is ready to go when you begin paid or when it is time for you to declare your taxes at the end of the year.

After you have taken these actions, your Amazon Seller Central account will be created! You will not need to do anything further with your account until you are ready to begin ordering and listing products, at which point you will need the account to complete these parts of the process.

Chapter 6 Branding Your Product & Making It Stand Out

In this section I will be covering how you can create a 'brand' for your product which will develop brand loyalty in the long term.

Naming Your Product

Before you order your product, you will need to have a name for it - a brand that can be seen on Amazon, or any other channels/websites that you use. Here are some tips to come up with a great name for your product.

Don't get hung up: come up with a range of ideas, but it's important to not get too picky - just go with something that works!

Relevant to the niche: You should make sure that your brand name fits in with your niche and target audience/demographic.

Domain name: Ideally, you want to be able to purchase the exact domain name for your brand name, so this is something to check when picking a name. I recommend getting a '.com' domain.

Trademark search: Another important factor to consider is to make sure your product name is unique. Search for 'us trademark search' on Google and you will be able to check if your product name is infringing on other trademarked terms. On top of this, make sure that no other products on Amazon are using the same names or close variations.

Designing Your Logo

You will also need a logo to go along with your product brand. Here are some tips for creating an effective logo:

Clean and simple: Keep your logo simple and professional. This will also help when having your logo printed on your product. You want your logo to be easily seen and recognized. Think about how the logo will actually look on the product.

Quality: Make sure you create a high-resolution logo that will ensure that the logo is clean when it is finally printed. I recommend having a resolution of at least 1000 x 1000 pixels.

Packaging Design

You may decide that you want to have specific packaging designed for your product. For example, you could have a custom branded box/bag - this helps to set your product apart from competitors, and consumers love this!

How to get the design work done

The great thing is that you don't need any design skills - you just need ideas that someone else can bring to life. I get my logos designed on fiverr.com, but there are other sites where you can find great designers such as Up-Work and People Per Hour.

Creating a Brand for the Future

Creating a brand is much more than creating a nice logo and packaging. To create a solid Brand you need to build on this by creating a vision for customer experience, vision of your company etc. You need to be instilling your vision and brand to customers in order to create a long-term reputation for your company. Another factor to consider is whether the brand you create can be relevant to other products within the same category or a similar category. This way you will be able to cross-promote your products in the future to get free traffic.

Making Your Product Stand Out

On top of developing strong branding for your product, you will need to make your product stand out - and this is especially crucial in a competitive market. The way to do this is to make slight tweaks to your products in order to make it stand out from the competition.

The tweaks that you make to your product can be very simple, and the best way to figure out what tweaks to make is by looking at the reviews of other products.

Negative reviews: Look at the negative verified reviews of the biggest competitive products. Are there any trends? Is this something you could easily fix on the product?

Positive reviews: Can you combine all the positive features into your product? Work out what customers like in other products and try to improve on this in your product.

Once you have some ideas for improving the product, go ahead and reach out to your supplier to see if they can incorporate these into your products, and what the associated costs are.

Other ways to tweak your product

Bundled Packages: You also have the option to combine your product with another low cost product which will help your product add more value than your competitors. For example, offering low cost face scrubbers with a face cream product.

Bonus offers: Another way to make your product stand out of the crowd is to create a high quality bonus package with extra free complementary information that is relevant to your product. For example, with many of my products I offer a free bonus eBook package that teaches people how to get the most of the product.

Choosing Your Final Product & Supplier

Choosing a Final Product

It's now time to start narrowing down and choosing a final product to make an order for. This can be tricky, so here are the criteria to go by to select the final winning product.

Profit: If one product makes more pure profit, then it is likely better to go with that product, but remember to take into account the other criteria that we have previously covered.

Opportunity: Does one product have a higher chance for growth than the other? Think about whether a product has other products that are complementary that you could also sell with your brand in the future.

Start-up capital: Very important - you need to choose a product that you can comfortably afford to finance. If one product is much more aligned with your budget and meets the other criteria, then I strongly suggest going with that product.

Although it's crucial that your product meets all the criteria, I also encourage you to take your gut instinct into account! Sleep on your product ideas and give yourself a bit of time to mull over them.

Choosing a Final Supplier

By now you would have spoken with a number of suppliers, but you will of course need to narrow this down to one.

Profit: Again, this is a crucial factor and you should sort your final supplier prospects by the total profit margins.

Quality: Make sure you obtain product samples from the supplier. Cross examine samples from different products. Does one stand out significantly? Try not to bias this decision by how much they cost. You can even do a blind test on someone you trust who doesn't know the cost of the products.

Your Experience with Suppliers: Consider how suppliers have acted when reaching out to them. Did they respond quickly and accurately? Did they have a good command of English? This is very important and will be especially crucial when progressing onto the next stages with them.

Operational factors: Compare the minimum order quantity, supplier ability, and lead-time between suppliers. The most important is lead-time - anything over 15 days can cause major issues, and can lead to you run out of inventory on Amazon.

By taking everything into account in this section, along with everything previously covered in the book, you should be able to narrow down to one product and one supplier. You are now ready to place your first order, and one step closer to building your highly profitable FBA business.

Chapter 7 Creating Your Product Listing

A crucial part of building a successful FBA business is having high quality and high converting product listings that stand out from the competition. You need to start building your product listing page while you are waiting for your product to be manufactured and shipped. This way, as soon as your product arrives into the Amazon fulfillment center you will be ready to start selling with a listing page that crushes your competition.

Keyword Optimization

Understanding the keywords that your customers are using to find your keywords is the most important step in optimizing your product listing page. These keywords will need to be in the product's title, description, and marketing strategies to efficiently drive the most traffic to your product.

Choosing your keywords: In order to discover the keywords that people are using to search for your product, there are key places to look and utilize.

Amazon Search Field - If you type in a product into the Amazon search bar and do not hit the enter key, you should see a list of suggestions for phrases to type. These are your keyword ideas for your products.

Here is an example for the jump rope product - along with your search you see multiple phrases that are related. Go ahead and write these down in a spreadsheet, as these will be very effective keywords to target in your product listing.

Google Keyword Planner

This is a great tool that anyone can use to find loads of keyword ideas that are related to your product. Simply sign up for an AdWords account and you can use the tool for free. Enter your product into the search bar and you will be provided with hundreds of related keywords. Pick and choose the ones that are most relevant to your product and then add these to your spreadsheet of keywords.

Your Competition

Most of the keywords for your product will be placed in title, bullet points, and description of your competitor's product listing ad. Narrow down all the keywords that they are targeting, are there any particular phrases that might not be the exact wording of your product but relevant? Start off with analyzing the top product in your niche, and start adding these to your keyword spreadsheet.

Fiverr

There are plenty of search engine optimization (SEO) specialists available to hire on Fiverr. If you hire one for a gig, they will be very effective in providing a targeted list of keywords for your product. This will save you time and it is definitely worth the small investment.

So go ahead and put in some work to put together a list of highly relevant and targeted keywords. This will effectively pave the way for starting to construct your product listing page.

Product Title

I will now be showing you how to craft the perfect title that will incorporate your targeted keywords, and draw in your targeted audience. Your product title is one of the most important aspects of your product listing page, which is why it is extremely important to optimize it. The product title is also a key opportunity to make your product stand out from your competitor's titles.

Product title details - Amazon titles need to be less than 200 characters. It is also important to know that Amazon will randomly grab keywords from your title and then include these in the URL for your product.

Product title tips:

Include your biggest primary keyword at the very beginning of your product title. This is very important for showing maximum relevancy to Amazon, which will help your product rank better in the search results.

Try to include as many other keywords in your title that you discovered and included in your spreadsheet when doing keyword research.

You do not need to repeat keywords in your product title. For example, if you have "Jump Rope Set" as your primary keyword, you do not need to add the keyword "Jump Rope" into your product title. Amazon will be able to detect the keywords within longer keywords and rank your product for all of those keywords.

Write for your customers! Although your product title needs to include as many of your targeted keywords, the title still needs to read well and be enticing for people to click on.

Follow the template below to create a very effective title for your product that will get your product ranked and convert sales.

A Perfect Title Formula:

Main Keyword - Other Relevant Keyword - Benefits & Features - Sales Copy

Make sure you use punctuation to make sure the title flows and reads well. The sales copy that you include should be a call-to-action, special offer, or a guarantee. This sales copy will convince customers to continue on to reading your product listing page. An example of this could be "#1 Jump Rope with Free Shipping".

So overall, use this formula create a product title that balances having enough keywords along with being readable to your prospective customers. Make sure you don't rush this - take your time to come up with a targeted and effective title that will pave the way for your sales!

Bullet Points

There is a bullet point section just below the price on your Amazon product page. Here you can add up to 5 bullet points that will highlight the crucial information that you want your customer to see. I certainly recommend utilizing all 5 bullet points as this is another key opportunity to get customers interested to read the rest of your product description.

Bullet point tips:

- Do your best to make the bullet points stand out. This can be done by using stars, capital lettering etc.

- Include the benefits of your products, not just the features. What are the main benefits of your product that your competitors' product may not offer?

- Highlight any special offers or bonuses that you have.

- Customers will always look at this section as it is just near the price. Use this as an opportunity to really sell your product to them!

- Don't forget to include your keywords in the bullet points. This will further help you to rank for your desired keywords.

- The first and the last bullet points are where the customer will look most. Use these to highlight your main benefits and offers.

Chapter 8 What Are the Best Ways to Launch Your Products?

Reviews Are Extremely Important

One of the most influential factors when it comes to sales are the reviews. If optimizing and advertising play a decisive role in making the product more visible and boosting the rankings, reviews are responsible for increasing the conversion rate. Shoppers are constantly looking for information regarding a merchandise, after all. Having a well-structured product description is a big plus because the buyers can find important details related to the goods, such as specifications and a nicely written description. If you can write it as a story, that is a bigger bonus. What they also want to find is the opinion of other buyers regarding your product. The reviews are valid social statements connected to your merchandise; in many cases, the shoppers consider them the most trustworthy. A few things that you can see in a customer's feedback are:

- user experience
- shipping
- quality of the product

The specialist reviewers like to write them as a list of advantages and disadvantages. They usually cover the points mentioned above, primarily if the product is user-friendly and it meets the customer's expectation related to quality and design, along with the delivery process itself. As users pop on this platform with a clear intention to buy products, the reviews are most influential when taking the decision to buy a product, assuming that the description and specifications already meet the buyer requirements. The more feedback you get, the more likely your product will sell. The A9 algorithm sees the reviews as extremely important, and it indexes them accordingly. As soon as you get your first review, this will mean an impressive boost in rankings. If you conduct your business in a niche with less competition, around ten to 20 sales should guarantee a spot for your product in the first two pages. Some merchants realized the importance of the reviews and tried to obtain them "artificially" by paying individuals to write reviews of products. This practice is not accepted by Amazon because it creates a fake image of a merchandise in front of customers. They have extremely strict terms and conditions related to this practice, but you can still find some tools to get honest reviews. Customers come first in Amazon's view; that's why they are focusing on achieving their satisfaction and protecting them from products of poor quality. If shoppers always consult the reviews when buying a merchandise online, merchants should also do that to improve the quality of their products and services. By listening to your customers (and consumers of your competitors), you can adjust and customize your products and services according to the needs of your customers. Sales may win you some people once, but the customer service and the quality of your product will give you their absolute loyalty. If you consider Amazon Retail, most of their consumers only use this platform to buy a broad range of products. They do not need to look anywhere else because they are extremely satisfied with the services and products provided by Amazon. At a lower scale, this is what you need to aim for. Furthermore, respecting the "voice" of your customers expressed through the reviews can undoubtedly help you achieve this objective.

Find Something to Boost Your Initial Sales

Let's consider that you are completely new to Amazon and want to make good money by selling high-quality goods to different buyers. At this point, you have the listings prepared, your content is optimized with keywords used in a natural manner, and you have very artistic photos well-structured and informative product description. However, you are still missing that special something to trigger your first sales. You know that you will be charged anyway by Amazon for your inventory, regardless if you make sales or not. As you are on this platform to sell goods, you can't afford to lose time so you need sales to start kicking immediately. In order to achieve this objective, besides optimizing your content, you will need to consider using Amazon Advertising to generate your first sales, particularly the Sponsored Products ads campaign. This involves setting buying special spots, which are extremely visible on the first page of results. It's also called Amazon PPC because you will place your product in that special spot, and you will pay for each click being made on your product. Since users are most likely interested to buy, they don't fool around when clicking on such an advertisement. If they like what they see, they will definitely buy a product. You need to set up your daily budget as well, which will cover a limited amount of clicks. This tool is your best chance of getting your first sales, making your first money on Amazon, and starting your journey to the top of the rankings.

Amazon Coupons

It's really hard to refuse a product that comes with a discount, especially when you are already interested in it or it is similar to the items that you are into. An interesting sale strategy is to have the first products sold for a lesser price to attract more shoppers towards your product. Of course, you merely can't sell all your existent inventory at a reduced rate; that's why it's important to set a limited amount of items that you want to sell for a discount. This a good way to make potential customers aware of your brand's merchandise. Traffic on Amazon can also be generated by external sources, such as your social media or business website. You can post an ad on Facebook or send customized emails to your customers from the database that you already have to announce your presence on Amazon and give them special offers. You can sweeten the deal by throwing in an Amazon coupon that's designated to provide a discount on one of your listed products on the platform. If you are hoping to get your first sales using this process, and let's say you have a few Amazon Coupons to give away, then you need to work intensively on this marketing campaign. After all, your presentation will need to reach more and more potential customers to become very effective. It's only up to you to choose your default sales trigger - whether you want to advertise through social media, send plenty of emails to your existing customers, give away discount coupons or choose the Amazon PPC option. Advertising on the platform can reach a higher number of customers compared to using external sources and offering coupons.

Follow Up to Get a Feedback

The most effective sale is the one that generates feedback because it creates all the necessary conditions to climb up on rankings, increase product visibility, and eventually generate other sales. In the old days of trade, sales were done through recommendations as well. The "word of mouth" was spread, and more and more people were aware of a specific product and its advantages. Sales triggered other sales, in other words. Things are about the same when it comes to online selling platforms, considering reviews and feedback are proven methods to produce more sales. The ideal situation is to get either after every sale, but it is genuinely hard to think of a seller which has achieved this performance. Reviews and feedback boost the popularity of the product and brand awareness, and shoppers are most likely to buy famed items because they are already considered trustworthy. A piece of good advice is to follow up with the customer to find out what he or she thinks about the merchandise. In the eyes of the shoppers, after all, it proves that you care about them and that you are willing to go the extra mile to satisfy their needs. This is the way to get positive feedback and reviews, which is something that Amazon and the users that are present on this platform appreciate very much. Another good idea is to comment on a customer review directly, thanking them for their opinion.

Chapter 9 Packing and Setting Up Shipments To Amazon

Now that you've listed your items and had them setup for sale through Fulfillment by Amazon, it's time to prepare your boxes to ship. Do not skimp or skip anything during this process, as your success depends on your ability to follow Amazon's requirements to ensure everything goes smoothly.

Step 1. Clean Everything

If you're selling any used goods or new goods with dust on the boxes, you'll unfortunately have to take the time to clean them up prior to packaging and shipping them. This part can seem like a time waster, but sending dirty products to customers is an easy way to get poor reviews and lose future business.

Start by removing any price tags. You do not want them to know that you paid a fraction of the cost they paid. To remove any of the sticky residue, you can use products like Goo Gone or just a little rubbing alcohol if it won't damage the packaging. Be careful while removing labels and cleaning, as any imperfects will make the item appear used even if it isn't.

Step 2. Prepping Your Items

If the item is in retail packaging that's undamaged, you can easily leave it as is. If it isn't, you will need to box or bag your product before placing any barcode labels on them. It is recommended that you bubble wrap items before bagging them. Boxing items when it's unnecessary should be avoided, as the costs are much too high for little in return.

Step 3. Labeling Items

Labeling is the next important step. Per the earlier recommendation, Avery 5160 (30) size labels are perfect for this application.

To print your labels, return to your product inventory by logging in at Seller Central, and clicking "Products Amazon Fulfills" under the "Inventory" tab. This will bring you to a page with all of your products awaiting labels and shipping. From here, check the items you are going to ship, and then from the drop down menu above or below, choose "Print Item Labels."

The following page will show you the items, and at the bottom is a drop down menu that lets you choose the printing method and label sizes. If you've chosen to use the Avery 5160 (30) sized labels, it should automatically be chosen as the default. Once you're prepared, click "Print Item Labels."

Here, Amazon will remind you that you'll be placing these barcode labels over the existing barcodes. If the barcode area is too small for your label, you can cover it with a white label and place the barcode elsewhere, but you MUST cover the existing barcode.

The result is a PDF that's downloadable, which you can then print. The barcodes should be easy to manage since they include the name of the item on them in most situations. If the item is cleaned and ready, place this barcode over the original barcode, follow the notes you took earlier concerning Amazon's requirements for packaging (remember, some items must be bagged or boxed per their requirements), and place it in the correct box for shipping.

Repeat this with all of your products until you're ready to ship.

Note that you can setup labeling by Amazon instead. This costs $0.20 per label, so it's a huge waste of your money since labeling really doesn't take very long at all. Only do this if you're selling massive quantities and really don't have the time or can't hire someone to help out.

Step 4. Shipping Your Box

Now that you've labeled all your items, fulfilled Amazon's requirements for packaging, and placed the items in the box securely, it's time to finally ship to Amazon for their fulfillment services. You've made it. This is almost time to celebrate a little!

Returning to your FBA inventory, you should be able to select all the items you've already labeled, and then from the drop down menu, choose "Send/Replenish Inventory."

Since we've already labeled and prepped our items, we can click "Review Shipments" on the follow page. This should tell you the places each item needs to go along with the name of the shipment. Note that you won't always be sending all products to the same distribution warehouse, so it's important not to package up your boxes before this step.

If you have more than a single shipment package on this page, you can click the "View contents" link beside each of the shipments to be made to see which products should go in which box. Package up your boxes as you go. Do not seal your boxes yet.

If everything is in the box where it belongs, choose "Approve Shipments," and you'll be able to purchase shipping for your packages. To finish this step, you'll have to weigh and measure your boxes, input this data into the shipping page, and select the appropriate carrier for the job. Most of the time, UPS is the route to go. Click "calculate" and Amazon will give you pricing and the option to print out your shipping labels.

You can simply tape your labels onto your boxes, but if you prefer adhesive printer paper, the best size for these box labels is Avery 8465, which has an adhesive label on each side of a standard sized sheet of printer paper. Once printed, remove both of the labels and place them on the box in a way that they cannot be sliced down the middle while it's being opened by Amazon's warehouse staff. Generally, the two top halves of the box are perfect. Take it to the UPS drop off, do a little celebratory dance, and start working on finding new products to continue growing your business. Amazon will let you know once your products have arrived and are ready for sale!

Chapter 10 Amazon FBA and Tax Season

Amazon FBA is a business that will require you to file taxes. You might be wondering how you can file taxes with Amazon FBA, including what tax forms you will need and what you need to track in order to submit your taxes clearly and precisely. In this chapter, we are going to summarize what needs to be done come tax season for you to properly file your Amazon FBA business so that you are compliant with what is required of you as a business owner.

When it comes to filing taxes for your Amazon FBA business, it is truly not that challenging. If you have ever filed as a self-employed individual before, you will be pleased to find that it is not much different than filing for your own business. If you are new to filing for yourself, you might want to book with a tax agent who can help you file your taxes properly so that you do not make any mistakes in your filing process.

Using the Amazon 1099-K Tax Form

1099-K tax forms are forms that help the IRS know how much money you have made monthly, as well as annually, through your business. Individuals who are filing on their own will often file 1099-K forms to track their income through their own businesses. Fortunately for you, Amazon also uses the 1099-K to track information relating to sales, taxes, and shipping fees. This means that if you are a professional seller who is selling large quantities of products through Amazon, your form will already be filled out through Amazon's employees as they manage your products. All you have to do, then, is print off the 1099-K and use it to file your taxes.

If you are an individual seller, or if you do not make a significant amount through your business in any given year, chances are you will not receive a 1099-K because you did not make enough money through your business to file it. For the 1099-K, there is a threshold of $20,000 that needs to be met in order for Amazon to fill it out. If you do not meet that threshold, Amazon will not fill it out for you, and you will not receive one.

It is important to realize that if you have more than $20,000 in sales, Amazon will be filing a 1099-K form for your business, which means the IRS already knows that you have a business with Amazon. If you fail to report this income or if you report it incorrectly, you could be audited due to your discrepancy. Pay attention and make sure that your numbers match the ones on the 1099-K generated by Amazon so that you do not find yourself being audited.

As well, even if you do not receive a 1099-K, you still must file taxes on all of the income that you received from Amazon. It will still count toward your overall annual income, and it just won't qualify you for a 1099-K to be filled out and provided to you from Amazon.

What Qualifies as Income

The IRS is going to track your gross annual income through Amazon, which is going to include everything that you earned, including your revenue, not just your profits. Any numbers relating to your income, including shipping charges and anything else you receive, are all going to be listed on your 1099-K, even if you did not receive all of these funds directly into your bank account.

If you are not sure about the numbers, or if you have never filed this way before, filing with a consultant can help you keep track of your numbers more effectively so that you do not make any mistakes and pay for it later on. Always trust the numbers that come in on your 1099-K because, at the end of the day, Amazon was responsible for helping you with all of the income, which means that their state-of-the-art systems are likely more accurate than your own.

Reporting Income Outside the US

If you are selling on Amazon outside of the US, you are not liable for US taxes, which means that you are not going to receive a 1099-K form from Amazon. What you will need to do is provide a W-8BEN form to Amazon which is going to exempt Amazon from having to report your income for tax purposes.

For anyone selling outside of the US, you are going to have to track your own income and file according to your country's unique tax laws. Again, it is still important that you report and pay taxes on your Amazon income as not doing so could result in serious penalties for lying on your taxes.

Tracking Amazon Tax Deductions

Anyone who runs their own business qualifies for certain tax deductions throughout the year. Typically, any expense that contributes to you running your own business is going to be considered a tax deduction, so it is important that you keep all of your receipts relating to your business. Keep receipts from everyone, such as your suppliers, your shipping companies, Amazon, and any promotional or marketing expenses that you pay. Anything that directly contributes to you making an income on Amazon can be considered a tax deduction, so feel free to note this down in your taxes.

It is important that you keep the receipts for any tax deduction that you make on your business. Receipts provide evidence that these funds were spent and that you did put the money toward running your business. If you do not have them, even if the money was spent on your business, you might run into problems later on should the IRS decide to audit you. Avoid these problems by keeping your business receipts for seven years so that any audits made are able to be proven and reported through your saved receipts.

Chapter 11 Tools That You Will Need to Get Started

You already know what Amazon FBA is. Let us have a quick brief of the process again. If you are a seller, you need to list your products for sale on the website of Amazon with a well calculated price that benefits you as well as the Amazon. Then, you have to ship your merchandize to the warehouse of Amazon. When a customer makes a purchase of your products, they get the shipping from Amazon and the company also handles the communication with the customers. And Amazon profits by charging a cut from the sale and a small amount of fees. The process will keep on running unless you want to stop it.

To get into flow with this business with Amazon, you must have some essential things handy. These supplies and tools will make your business easier and you will also earn more with time. However, it is not necessary that you must procure these tools in the beginning of your business. Moreover, many of these tools are tax deductible. Thus, you can take the help of these tools for last minute tax deductions. That is good news! Isn't it?

1. Inventory lab

Inventory lab is a web application which runs separately from your internet browser. Though it can work with any operating system and computer, it is recommended that you use it with at least Internet Explorer 8 and a modern browser. The application will support your work in terms of innovation and customer service. Inventory lab is capable of handling monthly profit/ loss, goods sold, etc. The additional

Scanning Application of Inventory Lab is also listed in the list of essential tools at #2!

2.   Scoutify

This application deals with scanning of items you list on Amazon. You will find Scoutify as a part of the previous application, Inventory Lab. The user interface of Scoutify is very simple to navigate. You will also find many features that will make your scanning portion of the business simpler than ever before. One exciting feature of the app is that if you receive multiple results after scanning an item, you do not have to scan the product again. You can simply go back to the results to verify the duplication of results.

3.   Gummed Tape Dispenser

An efficient tape dispenser is indispensable when you are working with someone as big as Amazon. Your customers will be pleased when they see the product packed in a professional manner. The recommended product to buy is Better Pack 333. The product is a gummed tape dispenser. Recall the kind of tapes on the packages of Amazon. This tape dispenser gives you the same kind of tapes. You will need only one portion of tape on both opening of your box. The dial on the tape dispenser gives you the perfect tape each time you enter the size of the tape required.

4.   Scan-Fob 2006

It is a 1D barcode scanner that you can hold in your hand and use it conveniently. It can be used to send data to various devices like iPhone and Android devices. This wireless Bluetooth laser barcode scanner lets you scan the barcode from a much longer distance than you expect. Thus, you do not have to take down every item from the top shelf of your garage to scan the barcode. It sounds superfluous but it really makes your business easier.

5.   E-bates

E-bates is a Cashback website and helps you a lot in online arbitrage. You can install it in your browser bar which will constantly remind you to activate cash back if you are working on a retail website. E-bates is more reliable in terms of giving you Cashbacks in time, which many other Cashback websites do not do.

6.   Self-Sealing Poly Bags

If you are dealing in smaller items like health and beauty items and groceries, you will definitely need a lot of self-sealing poly bags. You must keep bags in 4 sizes handy- 8_10, 9_12, 11_14 & 14_20. You can get 100 of each size of these bags from Amazon itself.

7.   Price Blink

If you want help with online sourcing, this tool is indispensable. You can add it in your browser bar and it will let you know about a product that you are searching for, if it is available for lower prices on other websites. Thus, you can also search websites that are not very popular for options of buying. It also notifies you of the coupon codes for the websites which you are currently using. Price Blink comes absolutely free!

8.   Dymo Label Writer

Dymo label writer is a very efficient solution for professional labeling, mailing and filing needs. You will save a lot of time with this tool at your disposal. You just need to connect this label writer to your computer and you can print labels directly from Outlook or Microsoft Word and many other famous programs. The thermal printing technology of the product eliminates the expense of toner or ink. You can also print expiration dates on grocery items and do many more things with it. Look for this product in a yard sale to save money.

9. Laser printer

A printer is an equally indispensable tool like a scanner. And, if it is a laser printer, nothing like it! It prints your papers quickly and saves you a lot of money since you do not have to buy ink frequently. You can even buy a wireless printer if your pocket allows. There are a lot of things to be printed in a business and a printer makes your business simpler.

10. Scotty peelers

They come in handy, really handy if you deal with liquidation products, or cut down boxes, or open cartons of online sourcing; which is quite obvious that you will do in Amazon FBA. You can even buy multiple Scotty Peelers and you will never have enough of them. The metal peelers are better than the plastic ones.

11. Amazon seller app

You can use this app to find out the probability of profits when you are making a purchase. It gives you comprehensive information about the number of sellers for the item that you are planning to list, the sales rank or if Amazon itself is selling the product. Thus, it helps you take a better decision in all aspects.

There are of course many more tools than those on the list. But, these are the essential things that you must have if you are going to start your Amazon FBA.

Chapter 12 Make Your First $1,000 On FBA

Following my story with getting my toes wet in FBA and making a huge amount of mistakes, it seems wise to give you a plan of action to make your first $1,000-2,000 on FBA. Hindsight is always 20/20, and this is how I wish I had started things off because it would have taught me all the lessons I learned the hard way.

Step 1. Gather Supplies, Sign Up, Upgrade to Professional Plan

We've went over all the items you'll need to get started, so begin there, and while you're waiting for items to ship or once you're ready to move forward, sign up for your seller account and download the Amazon Seller app. Upgrade to the professional plan on Seller Central. It will cost you $40, but for this plan to work, we really want to sell more than 40 items anyway.

Step 2. Clean Out Your Closets

For your first $1,000, at least part of this should simply be items around your house that you don't really need. This includes DVDs, CDs, records, video games, books, electronics, anything you got for Christmas but never used, etc. This should make up at least a roughly estimated $250 of your first $1,000. Use the Amazon Seller app to scan these items, and use the revenue calculator to estimate your earnings. If you can't make it to roughly $250, you'll need to overcompensate a bit on the next steps.

Go ahead and list these items for sale. If there are enough to bother with a shipment, ship them for fulfillment, and the earning will begin while you continue.

Step 3. Hit the Ground Running with Retail Arbitrage

While I think most successful FBA sellers eventually move away from going into every store and scanning anything that seems to be on sale, this really is the best way to start out. The risk/reward is lower than trying to jump headfirst into wholesale.

Where I live, this would mean going to the SPCA thrift shop, Goodwill, Walmart, Target, Lowes, Home Depot, Big Lots, Ross, TJ Maxx, Kohls, and many others. If there is a shopping center around, starting here is great since so many stores are located together and don't require a ton of gas or time simply traveling around. Outlet malls are even better.

Do not buy anything that cannot be sold at a price of three times the amount you've paid for it. You won't always have time to calculate actual profits while you're shopping, so this rule of thumb is your best bet to avoid losing any money on products that aren't worth selling.

This process could take a few days, but you should be able to calculate another opportunity for earnings of at least $250, if not significantly more.

Step 4. Facebook, Craigslist, Free Stuff

You should be shopping Craigslist pretty religiously. Not only can you sometimes find great deals, but you can also post ads for certain items that you believe will sell. Additionally, there are a lot of free listings on Craigslists, and while many of the items may not be worth a ton of money, they are free, so if they're viable to sell, the cost of shipping isn't really a huge concern. Try to take advantage of these while remembering that light items are better to sell than heavy items.

Unless you live in the middle of nowhere (and sometimes even if you do), you likely have a handful of Facebook groups that service people buying, selling, and trading in your area. Take advantage of these as well. Much like Craigslist, you can post ads for the types of things you'd like to buy and resell.

This method should easily be able to bring in an additional $250 worth of profit in products.

Step 5. Yard Sales and Flea Market

On the weekend, get up early and make your way to any yard sales and flea markets you can. The generally low prices at these sales are going to make for a lot of easy profit if you find anything decent. If you find a box or pile of items you might be able to sell, try to buy the entire thing for a deeply discounted rate.

For example, if someone has a nice selection of roughly 50 DVDs priced for $1 a piece, offer them $25 to take them all off their hands at once. This particular example works well at yard sales. The worst they can do is tell you, "No thanks," and if you're lucky they'll meet you somewhere in the middle.

If there are any multi-family yard sales or church rummage sales, you absolutely should be attending them. These tend to have lower prices and great amount of variety.

Again, you should fairly easily be able to net the remaining $250 worth of profit from products through this method. In fact, if you've done all four of these methods for sourcing products over a two-week period, I'd be surprised if you didn't end up with more than $1,000 worth of profits should everything sell.

Step 6. List and Ship to Amazon, Wait for Profits.

Anything that hasn't been listed and shipped to Amazon, go ahead and do that now. If you haven't reached an estimated worth of $1,000, just repeat the steps above throughout the next week, and you should be able to make up the difference.

Step 7. Take Notes

This is really the importance of the "your first $1,000" exercise. Your first $1,000 is just a small milestone in a long list of success stories you will have. What you learn from non-discriminately shopping pretty much every local resource available is that what seems to work for you may not be what works for others. Which of the items that caught your eye were actually extremely viable? Which ones sold immediately after the listing went live, and which sat around (or remain in storage still)? All of this is important because for your next $1,000, you will now know what to ask for when you post ads on Craigslist to buy stuff. You will also know what to stop and look at when you're browsing through a yard sale, which stores seem to produce well for you, and you're beginning to learn how to interact with people through social media in a laid back but semi-professional manner. Ultimately, you may have worked pretty hard for that first $1,000, especially in regards to time, but the information you learned along the way is the real payout.

Chapter 13 Delays

In regards to possible delays, it is fair to mention that you should be aware right from the beginning, even at the stage of supplier research.

You might be having a Friday afternoon, and feel like contacting your first suppliers to see how they respond, and you might not get any reply for a week from any of them. Instead of giving up the whole supplier research or thinking about what did you do wrong, you might be better-off looking up the Chinese calendar first.

In China holidays might differ according to where you live, and you should not only be aware, but also understand what they mean, and respect that.

I personally even write them messages like; have a good rest while on holiday and to all Factory workers too, but it's not necessarily at all.

Some of these holidays are not really chosen, but due to the Government, it's been forced on everyone to shut down all the factories.

Holidays can cause issues at both end of the Businesses, the factory and you as an Amazon FBA seller. When you place an order, make sure you don't run out of stock.

As you see sometimes, production might delay for a week or two. If you are not prepared properly, once you have no inventory at Amazon, you will lose your ranking, as well as loose profit, and many customers who might go buy a similar product. And next time they may buy the same other brand rather than look for you to know if you are back in stock.

Chinese holidays are important to take note of. There are also times that huge events take place in China that you should also be aware of, as some of them can even kill your business like many Amazon FBA sellers experienced when the Olympics took place in China in 2008.

The pollution is very high in China, so anytime a big event takes place, the Government takes extra measures by closing most factories in order to have a better looking sky.

It doesn't really matter where you source from, however you should watch the news and understand external causes of possible delays.

In regards to AIR shipping there are few days of delays that I have experienced, literally 1 or 2 days. It happened with DHL, as the Duty had to be paid before delivery, and I had to reschedule the delivery. I wasn't able to reschedule for Saturday, so I had to wait from Friday till Monday, knowing that my product was sitting at DHL's ware house since the Friday afternoon instead of me actually doing my quality checks.

Sea shipping will always take at least 4-6 weeks, if you source from China to the US, and possible delays might take another week or two.

Also, when sourcing by Sea Shipping, same as Air Shipping, Duties must be paid before picking up your shipment, or sending a freight forwarder for collection, and that is the most convenient option.

Also when importing with Sea Shipping, there are some busy times where public holidays could cause port congestion and your shipment could be delayed.

Always communicate with your suppliers to avoid any possible delays, as you might not have experienced. However, your supplier might be able to suggest good times for shipping, since they may know more about local news and Shipping Agencies than you.

Clearance paperwork can also cause delay before your product is released. So it's a good idea to be ready with all the documents that is required for this purpose on time, and make sure there are no errors on any of the documentations that you will provide as all that might just cause you additional delays.

In a perfect situation, to be able to source from any country to another should take no time, however there are so many steps, and so many companies are involved that for most of them you or your supplier are not special at all, and if they find something incorrect or against their procedure, it will cause a great loss of money to your Business.

Chapter 14 e-bay Vs. Amazon

Usually, there is no competition between the two platforms. The real thing is dependent on you and what you really want. This might sound somehow strange, so let's take a knife to it and break it down.

eBay

Over the years, eBay is like one mighty flea market, the sellers are doing most if not all of the jobs, like setting up your 'stand.' You will handle transactions, offer product, ship it, and perform all the things involved to make sales and purchase a complete chain. You have a 100% responsibility here.

The reason why this chapter begins with 'it's up to you' is that though it seems like a lot of work, there are benefits in it. One of the advantages is that you will earn more when you are doing more of the work. A larger percentage of the profit will be completely yours, or you will be having more of it than in a situation where someone else or a team is handling it for you.

Amazon FBA

We aren't looking at Amazon as a whole but Amazon FBA specifically. So how does that look like in the setting we are talking about?

This is like one big mall where you own a shop. There are storekeepers who work for everyone and help them sell their items. Once you sign up for the program, you will get a space in the warehouse. You will pay for it of course, but it also means that when you are at home sleeping or watching your favorite show, some is handling shipping, packing and delivering your items to your buyer's location.

Of course, the benefit is more than that, and we have explained most of it. The most important one we should talk about here are the charges you will pay for using the services.

Well, you can sell on both channels using Amazon.

You haven't forgotten Multi-Channel Fulfillment, have you? You will keep your item with Amazon, and they will do the job of shipping and delivering the item when people make an order on Amazon or on the other platforms.

Go to your seller account. Choose to create Multi-Channel Shipment to a channel like eBay. Let Amazon fill the submitted orders. They will also manage the orders you have submitted. Things will even be easier if you are using a professional account. Amazon can automatically fulfill the FBA inventory with MCF.

Chapter 15 How to Use Seller Central To Upload Inventory, Create Shipping Plan, Get Paid, and...

Using Amazon Seller Central is not that complicated as it seems to be. Let us see how you can use it.

Using Seller Central to get Payments
For initiating transmission of funds to your bank account from your seller account, Amazon Payments needs:

- Valid information of your credit card for billing and verification purposes.
- Valid information concerning your bank account to which you want the funds to be transferred.

After a sale takes place, and you confirm with Amazon that you have shipped the order, Amazon starts the process of payment from the account of buyer. However, in the case that it is an Amazon FBA order, Amazon will credit your account once they shipped out the order. The net proceeds of the sale are credited to your account. It is also important to note that the refunds to customers and selling fees are debited against the funds credited to your account.

The payments in your seller account are credited every 14 days. Amazon transfers the funds once Amazon Payments deduces that your funds do not need to be held to cover the charges, A-to-Z guarantee claims, refunds or other declarations against your transactions of sales. For receiving payments, you must mention the details of a US checking account/ UK bank account/ Eurozone bank account (Austria, Cyprus, Estonia, Belgium, Finland, France, Greece, Ireland, Germany, Italy, Luxembourg, the Netherlands,

Malta, Portugal, Slovenia, Slovakia, and Spain)/ New Zealand, Australia, India, Canada or Hong Kong.

When you need to ship your orders yourself
Amazon handles all the packaging, labelling and shipping on its own for your Amazon FBA products. But if you are working under the process of Amazon Merchant Shipping, you have to handle the shipping yourself.

Shipping, managing and selling your products
You can put buttons and allow clicks on your websites to sell your merchandize. You can check your requests and orders daily with the help of "Manage Orders" in Seller Central. You must ship the orders as soon as possible to gain customer loyalty.

Confirm the shipments
You need to confirm your shipment with Amazon and tell them the details of date of sending, the carrier used and other tracking information regarding the package. If you confirm the shipment, Amazon charges the customers. And, if you do not verify the shipment, your payment will not be initiated. The order is cancelled if you do not initiate the shipment after 30 days of order. You must sign in to Seller Central often. A notice will be displayed on the home page if any of your orders are in danger of cancellation.

Inventory Loader
If you want to upload multiple listings in one file to match against existing pages of products, you have to use Inventory Loader at Amazon.com. You cannot use it to create new pages of products. You can add new stock, amend existing items, and delete or "zero" your stock for items that are not available. You can also cleanse and replace all your listings with one upload only.

Since you are only modifying your stock, you do not have to provide product data in complete detail as you would when you use a category specific file of inventory. You can also use Inventory Loader to upload and modify your listings in multiple categories of products at the same time.

Using Seller Central to create Shipping Creation Workflow

You can create your shipment to the fulfillment centers of Amazon with the following steps of shipping creation workflow:

- Place Quantity
- Put Products In order
- Label Products
- Preview Consignment
- Prepare Consignment
- Summary

First of all, you need to choose your products in the inventory you want to ship to the company. You can do it using the "Manage FBA Inventory" or "Manage Inventory" page of the Seller Central. Select the product you want to transport, choose Send/ Replenish Inventory from the drop down menu of "Apply to Selected Items(s)" on Manage FBA Inventory page. The next page of Send/ Replenish Inventory will require you to take the following decisions:

Make a shipping plan/ Add to an Open Shipping Plan: In case you have an existing shipping plan, you can choose the plan from the drop down plan after you select "Add to an Existing Shipping Plan".

Verify your ship-from address: The address you had entered can be used to ship your consignment. If you wish to edit it, you can enter a fresh ship-from address.

Select the type of packing: You need to select case-packed products or individual products.

After you are done with all these steps, select "Continue to shipping plan" tab to start your workflow.

Send your FBA Inventory to Amazon

After you are set to send your inventory to Amazon, the next step is to create a shipping plan. It is a list of items which you wish to send to the fulfillment centers of Amazon. Your seller account has a shipment creation tool, which makes it simpler to select the items you wish to send, your shipment method, the quantity of the products, whether you wish to label the products yourself or Amazon should do it. You can also procure printable shipping and product labels from the shipping creation tools along with the guidance to prepare your items for shipment.

Once you are ready with your shipment plan, you can start preparing and packing your items in order to ship them to the Amazon fulfillment centers. You can break your shipping plan into various multiple shipments, which are directed to different Amazon fulfillment centers. This brings your products closer to your customers in different regions.

Chapter 16 How to Create Bundle To Eliminate Competition

You cannot ignore the competition on Amazon even if you want to. There are many fast selling products on Amazon which can overtake your products if you become lazy and do not take the competition seriously. People often become tired of competing with the swarm of sellers on your product page of Amazon. You need to look for different ways to raise your margins and trade more products. If you aspire that you had something exclusive to offer on the website, you need to take one step ahead. You do not need to private label or import your products to stand ahead of the crowd. You just need to create your own Amazon bundles. You must be wondering what are Amazon bundles.

Amazon bundles are exclusive products which you build yourself by joining two or more compatible, existing products into one bundle. Retail arbitrage products can be bundled together. Wholesale products can be bundled together. Imported products can also be bundled. Moreover, you can also bundle together all the three kinds of products.

Bundling the products together is a very effective method to stay ahead, at least three steps, of the competition. You do not need to have a very high budget for creating bundles.

Use your present method of sourcing to create bundles

You can sell your bundle and earn higher margin since you have an exclusive product in demand. Sometimes, several units are sold in just one day. You can own the product page of Amazon and the Buy Box as well. This keeps you ahead of competition. You can also create high demand by creating bundles of seasonal products. Moreover, you do not have to look for new providers of products if you repurpose saturated inventory. All your products can be sold in all categories of Amazon even if you offer entry level bundles or premium bundles.

The hurdles with bundles

Creating bundles does sound great but it is not so simple. Every bundle is not created equally. Not any random products can be bundled and sold like that. They will not sell for sure. You need to know what products you should bundle together to make maximum profits.

Important things to note while creating bundles

You must create bundles of products which are in demand. Create the product page of Amazon correctly so that buyers can easily find it in their search. It is equally important to price the bundles correctly to hit on target. Overpriced bundles will not sell. Choose the correct goods to bundle together. If you do not know how to bundle goods, you must go through the guidelines of bundling by Amazon. Otherwise, your listings may be cancelled. Another most important thing is to pass your bundle through the test of profitability factor.

A perfect bundle is the one which gives maximum value to the customers and the products are complimentary to each other. You must read the *Amazon's Product Bundling Policy in Seller Central* before you proceed to create your own bundles. You will also need to buy your own UPC (Universal Product Code) to list your bundle on Amazon.

When a bundle cannot be called a bundle?

A multi-pack cannot be categorized as a bundle. For example, you cannot call eight pairs of white socks as a bundle. If a bundle is just a variation of the parent product, you cannot call it a bundle.

When you do not need to buy a UPC

If your products fall into the following categories, you do not require buying a new UPC. The UPC on the product itself can be used.

- Home & Garden

Kitchen & Dining

Bedding & Bath

Furniture & Décor

Appliances

Arts, Sewing & Crafts

Lawn, Patio & Garden

Home Improvement

Pet Supplies

Lamps & Light Fixtures

Hand & Power Tools

Bath & Kitchen Fixtures

Building Supplies

Hardware

Grocery & Gourmet Foods

Sports & Outdoors

Outdoor Recreation

Fitness & Exercise

Cycling

Fishing & Hunting

Boating & Water Sports

Outdoor & Athletic Clothing

Team Sports

Sports Collectibles

Fan Shop

Golf

All Outdoors & Sports

If your products fall beyond these categories mentioned above, you would require buying a new UPC in favor of your multipack.

Chapter 17 Understanding Amazon's Success

Chances are you're fairly familiar with Amazon from the perspective of a buyer. They sell goods from a multitude of companies, including individuals who list their own items, and offer everything from digital products like music and e-books to physical products like home goods, toys, video games, and almost anything you can possibly think of ordering.

As the name might suggest, Amazon is huge much like the body of water that it's named after. Every single month they average more than 65 million buyers. That's 65 million customers all spending money through one interface, on one website, every single month. A large part of their success has been marketing and fulfilling those marketing promises, such as secure shopping, comparably low prices, and perks like free shipping for orders that qualify. In addition, Amazon has such a large array of items that it can almost virtually replace the need to ever leave the home to shop.

The largest reason Amazon is successful is because they are customer-centric. They cater to the buyer. As businessmen have always said, "The customer is always right." Amazon has lived by this motto while still going out of their way to improve the seller's experience as well.

Why You Should Use Amazon as a Seller

While being a buyer-oriented online shopping experience means that the buyer is almost always going to be able to get the upper-hand in disputes and other exchanges, it is still of the utmost importance to realize that Amazon is often the best possible place to sell your goods online. This is true for a couple reasons.

Firstly, Amazon has locked down the concept of the all-encompassing online shopping portal, and taking advantage of its many ways to produce an income is well documented and relatively easy compared to creating an online store or other online service from scratch. Their one-stop shopping experience provides more than you can provide on your own website, and unless you're ready to invest millions of dollars and years of hard work, it's unlikely that you'll be able to effectively compete with them on your own.

Secondly, the costs of getting started are minimal when compared to setting up your own online sales channels. While it may be tempting to try to avoid Amazon's fees, the truth is that a higher sales volume on Amazon and the initial cost of startup and maintaining a seller presence is much more expensive than these fees will typically be. Even if you are going to start an online store yourself, not having an Amazon presence means lost opportunities to reach the largest number of buyers in the world. Since the costs are lower to start with Amazon, it's obviously the best choice to start here and work on expanding later if that is your goal.

New and Used

One great advantage of Amazon, for both buyers and sellers, is that they not only list items that are brand new, but they also list items that are in various conditions. Having the option to sell used (and sometimes even rare) items through a safe and secure platform like Amazon means that nearly anything can be sold or bought through the same platform. While the ability to price the items you sell (and see everyone else's pricing) means more competition, this isn't as huge of a concern as one might think. We'll talk about that more later.

Customer Involvement

Another great thing about Amazon is that with a large amount of customers comes a huge amount of people that are interacting with the website past the point of purchase. This extends past simply writing reviews, but these reviews are of the utmost importance.

Traditionally, a person would go into a store, look at a product, possibly get to handle it for a few moments, and then have to decide if the price tag fit their expectations and limited knowledge of the item. This not only takes a lot of time, but the results are lackluster at best. There are very few ways to decide if a $1,000 laptop is worth $500 more than the $500 laptop sitting directly next to it. This is especially true if their technical specs are relatively similar. The internet has improved this through the use of customer reviewers. When it comes to customer reviews, Amazon tends to have the most reviews available per product when compared to other sites. This is true because they have a huge customer base, but it is also true because Amazon actively encourages members to take the time to let others know if they were happy with a product or not.

This translates into more sales for products that review well with purchasers. Where a dedicated website for selling products may be able to provide a really well written review from the content creators, the huge amount of customers willing to post reviews on Amazon can sometimes lead to HUNDREDS of opinions on a product. Similarly, when a product is bought a lot, it is hoisted to the top of the best seller lists that Amazon generates based on automated algorithms. As a seller, this means that if you are looking to pick up products that are highly desirable, it is easy for you to determine what products (or at least what type of products) are being sold regularly. This customer involvement and automated calculations done by Amazon allows you some detailed insight into the market(s) you are most likely to venture into.

Next, let's discuss the difference between selling on Amazon and selling on Amazon using their Fulfillment by Amazon services.

Chapter 18 Quality Control

Quality control is something that you should always have in mind.

Confirming the product at your first order is only one little part when talking about quality control. In fact, you should be thinking about quality control already when searching for suppliers.

I already mentioned earlier that once you are searching for suppliers on Alibaba, you should always find out where do they supply the most and you can always ask. However, even before reaching out to them on Alibaba there is a click of a button that will give you a nice overview of the factory's main transaction history.

With this example I can already assume that it might not be a good idea to use this supplier if you want to sell the product in Japan or Germany.

Of course you might take the advantage of being the first who does it. However, the standards and people's requirements differ in many countries.

I am relating this example to quality control already as some products are considered to be a good quality in the US, but might be very low for the UK, or vice versa.

As for a supplier who provides low prices, and thinking that will make it on the US market, you should make sure that the main transaction history for the same supplier is indeed the US market.

Next, you should be ordering samples as I explained before by comparing multiple suppliers' product as well as making sure they are using safe packaging for delivery.

Once you have chosen the right supplier and already private labeled your sample product, you must be very vigilant and try to find as many mistakes as possible, faults, or defects right at the beginning.

In case there is a problem or fault with the OEM sample order and you assume that in higher volume those defects will disappear, then you really should think again.

Any careless attitude you display will reflect on your product, and your suppliers will never spend more money on your product, neither will they work harder unless you make them do so.

That being said, you must always exhibit an attitude towards your product like a real business, and always look at the quality, and if there is any direction you want to go it is only to create better and better quality, and your suppliers must be on the same page.

In order to make sure that your suppliers are always on the same page with you, everything must be documented, not only to remind them about your expectations, but to make sure they understand who dictates the terms in regards to the quality.

I do understand that there are some awesome employees out there who never required being baby sited; how-ever you can only be 100% sure if you really do everything in your power to keep it that way.

I don't mean to be iron feast, and you must appreciate the hard work they do for you, and should mention often that you are very happy with the factory. And when your business is going very well, you should show your face by visiting the factory workers. You can also take the factory manager out for a dinner, if you can afford it at least once a year.

Back to documentation, as that's one of the key things that you must practice at all times.

At first if you really want to make sure that everything goes well, you must have a plan for your first large order in regards to quality check. There are many suppliers that when they send out one or two samples they will make sure that it is very well presented. However, once you move on a high volume production you can experience faulty products, and it's vital to have a written plan in order to avoid conflicts that could happen.

There are multiple ways to achieve this; some might cost you lots, like hiring a third party inspection company. However, you might ask your suppliers to carry out self-inspections before shipping.

There is an excellent technique that I used at first, and even since then, and it's completely free. What you do is that you ask your supplier to provide pictures at each phase of the production.

1st Picture:
Once the product comes off the production line and still with no logo on it; It must be the right measurements as well as colours.

2nd Picture:
Once the product has been created, and your logo is visible on it. You might also order an English user guide that also

has your logo on it, which you might also want to see and confirm before shipping.

3rd Picture:
The product already in your OEM packaging.

4th Picture:
Once all products are in the box that will be shipped, while the box is still open

5th Picture:
Photo of the Box/Boxes that are now ready to be shipped, clearly visible with the shipping label.

All the above mentioned must be confirmed before placing the order and must be written on the Sales Agreement / Purchasing Agreement.

The reason is that you have to understand that mistakes can be made by your supplier, and it's your responsibility to spot them as early as possible in order to minimize your cost.

An example here is you spot a fault when it comes off the production line, when there is no logo on the product, it will cost lot less to the factory to improve it. However, once they do the screen printing on all 100, or more units, that will be more cost to them and more delay to you.

Stage 2, once there is logo on the product, and you might spot that the logo is not positioned the way you want, or they have used the wrong colour, you must tell them that right then. And you should proceed the same way in regards to the packaging, as well as with the user guide in case you will have that.

Let's say that your products are already shipped to you, and you receive it with all above mentioned faults, you might choose to send it back, but that will cost you so much, and probably your suppliers will not take it back anyways... Or try to sell it that way at a cheaper price, hoping someone will buy the faulty products, or you might as well just bin them.

The worse that can happen is that you didn't spot any of the faults but customers receiving the products did. This can be very bad for your reputation and you will have difficulties creating a good name for your brand.

I hope all that makes sense. Also realize there are plenty of tasks to do, but believe me all this little steps matter in order to be successful, especially if you want to sell your products on Amazon.

Chapter 19 Instagram / Facebook Hacks

Instagram

Instagram is a social media platform where not only can you upload your pictures and very short videos that you personally took, but also edit them with various filters and borders, among other things. Even better, you can post on Instagram and share the same posts on 4 other social media platforms, including Facebook and Twitter, at the same time. Many businesses have started to shift to Instagram marketing for selling their products and services, simply because our minds tend to process information through sight (visuals) and sounds better. Some of the biggest names in the business that are actively marketing their brands on Instagram include Red Bull, Virgin America, Adidas, and Intel. And they do so in different ways.

Virgin America takes a less creative but nevertheless effective approach to marketing on Instagram. An example of this is how they promoted their first-class flights. They simply took photos of the immensely popular Pomeranian puppy named Boo on their flights and posted them on Virgin America's Instagram account.

Others, like Intel, take a relatively more creative approach to Instagram marketing. They market their latest computer processors not by showing pictures of the chips or processors themselves, which are very dull and boring to look at, but by posting well-edited pictures of the top computers that use those processors. By showing off the sexy computers that use the boring-looking chips, Intel is able to engage its audiences and promote their products more effectively by showing on which of the top and visually stimulating computer models their chips are being used in.

The credit card company American Express also takes a creative and indirect approach to promote its credit card services through Instagram. In particular, they don't post pictures of their credit cards - boring and very limited - but instead, post pictures of the activities and events that the company sponsors or has sponsored. They also make use of hashtags on their Instagram posts to position their financial services as being a necessary part of a fulfilling and modern lifestyle.

While you can upload short videos on Instagram, they'll be too short (maximum of 30 seconds only) to be meaningful. If you'd like to upload videos, better do so on YouTube instead. Instagram - for social media marketing purposes - is best suited for posting and editing great pictures.

And speaking of focusing on pictures, social media marketing on this platform isn't as simple as pointing, shooting, and uploading. It's a bit more complicated than that but not so complex that you won't be able to do it yourself. You have to strategically think about and choose the kinds of images you'll share on your brand's Instagram account.

After taking the pictures or images you determined will be best for your social media marketing campaign, you'll need to edit them to give them the most "oomph" and "wow" factor possible. You can edit them on the app itself, right before you post them. Instagram features several cool preset filters or you can customize them yourself using the app if you're familiar with photo-editing concepts. Doing this can turn "ok" into "great" and "ho-hum" into "wow"!

And lastly, you can optimize your image's contribution to your brand's overall social media campaign by coming up with really good hashtags. Doing so can help your images be easily categorized by leading search engines into specific keyword categories, and make them even easier to discover by others.

Other Instagram Best Practices

One specific way to do this on Instagram is to post images or pictures of the people that make up your brand or products and services. And that includes posting pictures of you! Doing so will give your brand a "human" face and something to personally connect to. And when people see the faces behind the brand or product, they're more likely to trust it, engage with it, and patronize it.

Another way to help your prospects and existing customers connect with your brand on a deeper level is to post images and pictures of behind-the-scenes stuff, like how your products are made and packaged, or how it looks like when you render the service you're marketing. Posting pics and images of things like this can help people trust your brand better due to a better sense of familiarity, i.e., they know what goes into your products, who the people rendering your services are, etc. Just be careful not to show too much info on the pics and images so that your competitors won't be able to copy you.

Because Facebook is the Goliath, the Leviathan, and the Paul Bundy of all social media platforms, there's no way you can lose when you promote your brand on these social media platforms. By the sheer volume of prospects alone, it's already worth the effort. But as your favorite infomercials would often say - but wait, there's more!

One of the biggest benefits of marketing on Facebook, especially through paid advertising, is the ability to target your market very specifically. How's that? You see, Facebook isn't just a vast social media platform. It's also probably one of the world's biggest, if not the biggest, database of personal information of billions of people all over the world! You may not be aware of it, but Facebook keeps track of your activities on the platform such as the things you liked, shared, FB accounts or pages followed, where you accessed your account, and so much more. Through such information, Facebook is able to profile you - and everyone else who uses it - with a high degree of accuracy. So Facebook knows who to shoot your content to according to your demographic specifications like age, gender, location, interests, etc.

You can take advantage of Facebook's vast membership, i.e., target market in 2 ways: free content and paid advertising. With free content, you'll have to build your brand's base of followers gradually over time. If you're looking for a longer-term and more economical option, this is your thing. But if you'd like to kick-start your brand's social media marketing and reach a whole lot of people immediately, paid Facebook advertising is the key.

With traditional advertising on print media, TV, or radio, you won't be able to specifically target your desired audience. It's because such forms of advertising are using what's known as a "shotgun" approach, meaning advertisements are thrown at masses of people without concern as to whether or not the right people will see it. That's why traditional advertising is also called mass media advertising. If it happens that most of the people who bought today's paper where you advertised your brand's product or service aren't your target customers or prospects, your advertising money would just go down the drain. Also, mass media advertising is expensive.

Advertising on Facebook is the total opposite of mass media marketing, though it can still reach a big mass of people. First, you have the ability to narrow down the people who would see your advertisement according to many categories such as age, gender, interests, and city among others. So unlike the shotgun approach employed by traditional mass media advertisements, you won't waste your advertising money on prospects that have no chance in hell of buying your products or availing of your services.

Another benefit of using paid Facebook marketing or advertising instead of traditional or mass media advertising is cost. For one, you have complete control over your budget on Facebook ads. You're not forced to toe the line of the advertising rates of traditional mass media outlets, but instead, you can set your own limit on advertising expenses on the platform. And even cooler is the fact that you can also allocate that budget across a specific time period. For example, you can set a budget of $70 for an advertising campaign that will run for 1 week, where Facebook will use up only $10 dollars of your budget daily for the next 7 days. Talk about the ability to control your advertising expenses, eh?

Facebook Marketing

To make the most out of your brand's Facebook marketing, be it paid or free, you must be aware of how things work on Facebook, particularly the platform's marketing practices. Don't think of these as ironclad regulations, but more like signposts or guidelines that can help you optimize your brand's Facebook engagements and conversions en route to higher sales.

Engage

The first thing to keep in mind is the primary goal of social media marketing, which is engagement. If you find it hard to remember most of the guidelines, then at least never forget that engagement is what it's about. Doing so will help you keep the other guidelines in mind.

Okay, going back to engagement, I want you to look at your favorite Facebook pages, whether it's those of your favorite celebrities or brands. Go ahead, put this book down and take a look - and observe. What do you see? That's right...they hardly ever sell directly! What they're doing is engaging you because they know that the higher their level of engagement is with you and all their other followers, the higher the chances of you buying something they're selling or promoting. Why? You don't feel like they're just interested in making you part with your hard-earned money. They make you feel you're an actual person!

So, when "selling" on Facebook, don't "sell" but engage.

If you want to really engage people, the best way to do so is to think as they do. By putting yourself in their position and thinking about what helpful or interesting content you can post on your brand's Facebook page and on its advertisements on the social media platform that they'll like and share. By focusing first on what your target market or audience wants and needs, you'll be able to connect with them, and even develop a relationship. Sales will just be a byproduct of those relationships. Remember, social media marketing is primarily an indirect form of marketing. Right!

Consistency

Another way in which you can effectively market your products and services on Facebook is through content posting consistency. What does this mean?

First, consistency refers to frequency. If you post once a month, your brand will eventually drift out of the consciousness of your audience members, i.e., your prospects and customers, because of the deluge of posts they're exposed to on a daily basis. Posting too frequently can also backfire, i.e., posting twice or thrice daily. So how frequently should you post on your brand's Facebook page?

While there's no hard and fast rule about it, studies have discovered that 3 to 5 times weekly is optimal in many cases, though it may be slightly different according to your brand's unique audience and circumstances. Consider 3 to 5 times weekly as a good starting point and adjust accordingly when needed as you go along.

Consistency also means being consistent with the quality of the content you post on your brand's Facebook page or advertisements. Don't post just for the sake of posting content - make sure whatever you post is of good quality and has a high potential for engagement. Remember that in social media, content is king.

The best way for you to ensure that you always post high-quality and engaging content is to think ahead - plan your brand's Facebook and other social media platform content in advance. That way, you have enough time to curate excellent content and the opportunity to see how all your content fits together to optimize engagement.

Chapter 20 Is Amazon FBA the Right Service for Me?

If you have a passion for buying and selling, the yes, Amazon FBA is the ideal business platform to consider. After all, since you already love online retail anyway, why not take it a step further and try to make some money out of it? With FBA, what you are doing is scouring for items (shopping) and then reselling them to other customers. Amazon has already made the job easier for you by taking away the worry about storage space, sales, shipping and customer support. All you need to do is find the products you are passionate about selling and get started.

Here is how you can tell whether Amazon FBA is the perfect online business and passive income stream for you:

- You are looking for a long-term side hustle that is dependable.

- You are looking for extra income aside from your regular 9-5 job.

- You want an additional way of making money online, but from the comfort of your home.

- You have always wanted to dabble in entrepreneurship without taking too much risk that is going to land you in debt.

In addition, Amazon FBA is not going to be the perfect business model for you if:

- You are hoping this is going to be a shortcut to getting rich quickly (no such shortcut like that exists, unfortunately).

- You are hoping to make massive profits in a short amount of time.

- You are looking for a quick return on the investment that you put in.

- You do not have the time to commit to doing the necessary work.

Quick Stats and Facts about Amazon's FBA Service

For those who are new to the Amazon FBA scene, here are some quick and important facts that you should keep abreast of. One, more than one Amazon marketplace exists and it depends on where your customers are located. A customer's location is going to determine which Amazon.com store they see. The location will also determine which fulfillment service your customers experience.

Picture 2

By far, Amazon's largest marketplace is none other than the United States of course, which also happens to be the most active marketplace compared to the rest. Amazon's marketplaces are divided into the following categories:

In North America, the marketplaces are:

- *Canada*
- *Mexico*

- United States

In Europe:
- *Spain*
- *Germany*

- United Kingdom
- *France*
- *Italy*

In Asia:
- *India*
- *China*
- *Japan*

Each marketplace's website address will reflect its location. Amazon in the UK, for example, is accessed via Amazon.co.uk. In France, the address would be Amazon.fr, in Japan it's Amazon.co.jp and so on. The location of each marketplace would determine the specific regulations and tax laws, which apply locally depending on the country and region, which you would need to familiarize yourself with before you set up your FBA business.

By default, for most sellers based in the U.S., the marketplace would, of course, be Amazon.com. However, sellers do have the option of branching out and diversifying their products into other regions if they wanted to. The advantage of doing that is you are expanding your services and potentially boosting revenue, but the downside is you might have to deal with higher costs when it comes to shipping. You will also need to have the time to commit to managing different stores in different regions. If you cannot, you will need to have the necessary funds to hire help in managing and operating your multiple stores.

Now, if you are happy just with running a simple retail store with no plans for expansion, then you will not need an e-Commerce website to sell on FBA. However, if you want to take your business a step further, then an e-Commerce store is the way to do. That decision would depend entirely on what your business goals are. One advantage of having an e-Commerce store operating outside Amazon is the opportunity to increase the visibility of your business and products, which means you are increasing your chances of selling more.

Several other reasons to consider an e-Commerce store include:

- More options to explore selling your products other than what is offered by Amazon.

- You get to implement various other strategies to scale your business.

- Opportunity to build on brand equity.

- Opportunity to increase your market reach through advertising.

- Opportunity to build a solid customer base.

- Opportunity to build an email list.

- Opportunity to generate B2B sales

- Better flexibility with products if it is your own website.

Benefits of Using Amazon as a Selling Platform

For an online business to be deemed a success, it needs to be efficient and fast when it comes to shipping (among other things). Amazon has already perfected this aspect into an unbeatable process, going the extra mile to ensure that their shipping is always top-notch. They have been doing this ever since Amazon first went live and they have only improved on their shipping service over time. A large part of why customers keep coming back to Amazon is because of their renowned ability to get their orders to customers in the fastest time possible, no matter where in the world the customer may be.

Among the primary reasons sellers want to do business on Amazon's platform is because when you sell on Amazon, you automatically open up to a huge customer base with a high conversion rate. This is something you are not going to be able to replicate on any other e-commerce platform, eBay included. You are able to make more money by doing less work than you normally would on other platforms. Amazon also offers significant advantages, especially for sellers seeking to reach a large and diverse clientele that is ready to spend money online, in a short amount of time.

Amazon has - and always will - put their customers first above anything. The company continues to strive to create better shopping experiences; even going so far as to try to improve their shipping times so they can deliver products even faster than what they are already doing. It also continues to work hard to improve the overall shopping experience customers get when they come to their website. When you sell on Amazon, you are selling with the best of the best. The other benefits you stand to gain include:

- *A Willing and Ready Customer Base* - Amazon's power lies in its large customer base, all of whom are ready and willing to purchase products that they need. By selling on Amazon, compared to many other retail platforms, the number of potential customers is more than triple the number of potential customers on eBay. This means you have an incredible opportunity in your hands. The chance to reach an ever-ready crowd, ready to buy online the minute they set up their business using Amazon. Sellers on Amazon can reach 237 million customers.

- *Customer Spending Power* - Customers love retail shopping. More importantly, they love retail shopping on Amazon more than any other platform. Amazon's revenue in June 2018 surged to $81.76 billion. Consequently, eBay reported $17.05 billion in that same period. An RBC survey even revealed that the average customer who shops on Amazon would spend approximately $320 annually. These numbers are very promising from a seller's point of view. It is an opportunity for sellers to gain depth and breadth where the visibility of their business is concerned.

- *Its Undisputed Reputation* - Amazon has a credible reputation. When it comes to credibility, no other platform can hold a candle to Amazon, thanks to its exceptional customer service and shipping. This has enabled Amazon to hold a large market share of online consumers simply because of their amazing services. This is something to keep in mind if you are deciding between eBay and Amazon.

- *The Power of Prime* - Amazon Prime can absolutely increase your revenues and increase the number of customers. With Prime, Amazon encourages customers to spend a little bit more by giving incentives such as two-day free shipping on plenty of Prime products. Prime customers spent an average of $528 a year compared to $320 spent by non-Prime Amazon customers.

- *Absence of Listing Fees* - While some platforms charge fees just to list products, Amazon does not. You will only be charged when you have made a sale. As a seller, this means you can list as many items as you would like on Amazon and then leave them until a customer has purchased them. The slight downside with this one is, the sales fee is rather hefty, with Amazon taking at least 20% of the profit. This fee is even higher if you are an FBA seller but of course, when you become an FBA seller, you are doing less work, therefore it balances out in the end.

- *No Relisting Needed* - A huge, hassle-free advantage that Amazon has over platforms like eBay is there is no need to continuously relist your items the way you would need to on eBay. Unless you sign up for the FBA service though, you are going to have to handle the shipping and customer service aspect of the business yourself.

- *You Can Charge Slightly Higher Prices* - Customers would be willing to pay the extra too, for the sake of the guarantee that comes with Amazon. Amazon, at the end of the day, is an online retailer. Like other retailers, they make their money by selling items at competitive rates. This process contrasts with that of a wholesaler, who charges you the lowest possible price, especially if you buy in bulk. eBay acts as a wholesale market and charges the lowest price. For example, a t-shirt may cost $15 on eBay but on Amazon, the same t-shirt might cost you $20. The reason for this increase is that Amazon sells new items (although there are used options available for certain products too), whereas eBay sells mostly used items.

- *Home of Reliable Brands* - Amazon stocks some of the most reliable brands on the market. As one of the most trusted retail names out there, Amazon and many of its customers are willing to pay $99 a year to be part of the Prime service. If you sell your products through Amazon, your business is then associated with a trusted brand. If you are a budding brand or the average online entrepreneur trying to make ends meet, Amazon is a good starting point. You get to access their large customer base while you learn the ropes of the business, before expanding to sell your products on shelves like Walmart.

- *An Excellent Learning Platform* - Business is a risk, but you can minimize that risk when you sell on Amazon. You can use the Amazon platform to test your target market for the products you plan to sell. By selling on Amazon, you gain access to retail data that enables you to see how your product is doing, what the demand is and what you can charge for your product.

- *Driving Awareness* - Amazon can be a great tool used to drive traffic to your other websites. Even better if you have a social media account or blog. It can be a valuable source of buyer information, which can give you great input on how to sell your products from what offers customers like, what they do not like, best times to open for promotions and so on. This should be part of your marketing strategy, to plan for long-term and sustainable success.

- *Perks of Amazon Associates* - You can take advantage of Amazon Associates services to market and promote products related to the industry on your website. Amazon Associates is an affiliate program that allows sellers to earn commissions through affiliate links. A slight downside with this option here is that there will be a clash of interest on the products you sell and the ones you promote. One way to avoid this conflict is by selecting products you promote meticulously and not burn your business.

- *Getting A Boost in Sales of 30-50%* - This boost primarily comes from Amazon's Prime program. Many shoppers do not like the idea of having to pay for shipping and Prime and stepped up to solve that problem. As a Prime user, you are entitled to 2-days of free shipping on any Prime-eligible products. This, in turn, increases the shopper's probability of purchases. Combine that with the "trust factor", where Amazon has built an undisputed reputation for itself and your sales are going to jump exponentially. When a customer sees the "Shipped by Amazon" or "Fulfilled by Amazon" indicator, there is a sense of relief and peace of mind. They know their products are safe and they are not going to be scammed, which is a very real probability if they were to purchase from an unknown merchant with no long-standing history.

- *You do not have to worry about Shipping* - You would be surprised at how tedious and time consuming the shipping and handling process can be. Once again, it is a huge relief for merchants, knowing that Amazon is going to take care of all of that for them. Amazon is the expert when it comes to shipping and they have gone to great lengths to ensure continued quality service, in the fastest and most reliable way. This gives FBA sellers a wonderful and must-not-miss opportunity to capitalize on that. Sellers get to save a lot of time and resources, which they would otherwise have to divert towards handling the shipping aspect. With that out of the way, you are left free and clear to focus entirely on advertising and marketing your products.

- *You Gain the Trust of Your Customers* - With products guaranteed to arrive, customers will love any business running under Amazon and its FBA label. It is not only Americans that love and trust Amazon either. Customers around the world have been turning to the retail giant for years to have their needs met. It is irrefutable what those three simple words *"Fulfilled by Amazon"* can do for your sales figures. Even if the customer has never heard of you until you, they will be completely comfortable purchasing from you, thanks again to the level of trust that is associated with Amazon. Shoppers are more likely to purchase from a retailer they know without a doubt that they can trust.

- *You are Automatically Eligible for Prime* - With 64% of American households being members of Amazon Prime that is almost 85 million customers who are currently using this premier service. Those who are members of Prime are *not* going to buy products that are not eligible for the Prime option. Having that Prime logo is tapping into the trust factor once again and when it comes to selling on Amazon FBA, Prime is definitely the way to go.

- *You Get Access to the "Buy Box"* - Amazon's "buy box" is the white box, which is located on the right, the same section where customers can click on the "Add to Cart" or "Buy Now" options. If you are wondering why this box matters so much, here is why. On Amazon, you will find two types of sellers. One is Amazon themselves; the second is third party. The latter category is made up of every company who is *not a part* of Amazon themselves. If you have your own eCommerce store, this is you. Now, several of these third-party businesses are going to be selling the same product, with the same details listed on their site. The sellers then, compete to win the "Buy Box", because, with this option on your page, you become the seller whose product is selected. Your product becomes the one customers add to their cart or buy now. 83% of sales on Amazon happen through the Buy Box option, which makes it a statistic you cannot ignore. In addition, yes, you have to "win" this option and it is Amazon who determines who the winner is. Amazon relies on an algorithm, which then determines the seller who will be represented in the Buy Box and for what duration. One thing's for sure, the Buy Box is going to give you a lot of preference as an FBA seller.

Chapter 21 Mistakes to Avoid

Not creating expandable brands and product lines from the start: If you are planning to build a sustainable business brand, you will want a larger umbrella of products to expand your business in the long run. Pick primary products that have plenty of complimentary purchases or can be bundled together with other items. This way you can keep adding items to create a longer product line under your brand. For example, if you zero in on the electronic gadgets niche, you may have a whole bunch of accessories and replaceable parts to sell to under a single business brand.

Go with bundled products and multi-packs if you are looking to score really big with Amazon FBA. Single items that sell are unlikely to be competition free or low competition on Amazon. Almost all products that sell reasonably well have tons of merchants in the category. Also, profit on one item products is swallowed by Amazon fees. Unless you can find a sweet spot between a high priced product that is also in demand and has low competition, you may not be able to achieve stellar results with single items.

Also, your woes will increase if Amazon sells the product. Unless you have a terrific edge, it is going to be hard to compete with Amazon. Bundling up products or creating multi-packs may require greater time or money. You need to source a variety of items and bundle them. However, it can be highly beneficial for long term profits.

Underestimating the holidays: As long as you are comfortable holding on to these items for roughly 10 months, the deals you can find on decorations during the days immediately after most major holidays can practically guarantee acceptable profit margins on nearly everything you can imagine. What's more, by waiting 10 months before sending them to Amazon, you minimize your storage costs while at the same time taking advantage of all the people who like to plan for the holidays early. Alternately, you can wait until just a few weeks prior to the holiday to post your products and raise the prices even more to grab customers who waited until the last second and as a result, don't care about the costs.

Another good place to look is in the autocomplete results of search engines on websites like eBay or Etsy, places where people are already going to search for harder to find items. In fact, if you ultimately find that the community for buying and selling related items is particularly robust, you may wish to consider starting a store on one of these platforms yourself.

Not listing products the right way

Even though we are told time and time again not to judge a book by its cover, shopping on Amazon, and anywhere online in general, is quite the opposite. One of the vital aspects of any listing on Amazon is the title, which informs potential buyers what the product is all about.

- Add keywords to the title to help the product to rank when buyers search

- Incorporate brand name

- Incorporate the name of the product
Add any features that distinguish the item

  - Its use

- Color

- Size

For instance, if you are selling a pacifier, an ideal title would look something similar to this: Deluxe Silicone Baby Pacifier – Easy for Parents – BPA Free – Set of 2 Pacifiers – Blue

Goals for an Amazon product title should do the following:

- Educate potential consumers about the product, even before they read the product page

- Add a few keywords to showcase the product and its use

Not taking full advantage of images: Another important aspect of the product details of items on Amazon is the images included in the listing. They can cause shoppers to click on your listing just because of the quality of the image. That's why you should spend a good amount of time to research images that are top-notch. Amazon product images should include:

- Showcase product size by having a human hold it

- Information images like charts

- Images that include features of the product and compare it to other similar items

- Images of your product being utilized

- The back label

- The item from all different angles

A great resource to find top-notch Amazon images for your listings that are also affordable is AMZDream.com.

Not using enough bullet points: If potential buyers fail to be swooned by your choice of title and images, bullet points are the next best thing to get a straightforward reaction. You have five spaces to include bullet points, but this doesn't mean you only have to use five words or even sentences. I personally use short paragraphs in each of those bullet points to home in on benefits and features of the item. Address common questions and objections as well. Use the first three points to showcase your products most pertinent features and use the other bullet points to answer common inquiries or customer objections.

Not pricing products properly: Opt to sell private label products that are priced above $10. Amazon lists items priced below $10 as "Add On Items, which means buyers cannot purchase your item by itself. They have to make additional purchases to be able to buy your product. Additionally, profit margins for products priced below $10 after deducting Amazon's fee can be rather low for building a lucrative, long-term business. You will need a very higher sales volume to witness recent returns. Ideally, pick products that sell in the range of $10-$30 for higher profit margins.

Few things will kill you like low cost products on Amazon unless you predict an unrealistically high sales volume. You may think inexpensive items carry less risk or are more frequently picked up by customers on impulse. However, selling products for below $5 is not likely to be profitable even with a high sales volume or next to nothing sourcing price. The shipping cost (to Amazon's warehouse) and fees will leave you with a few pennies.

Not treating it like a business: While Amazon FBA is not the same as having your traditional website up and running where you sell products to people, you should still treat the time that you spend on Amazon FBA the same that you would like an e-commerce business. Even though using Amazon FBA allows you to move away from creating your website, this does not mean that you should not take Amazon FBA seriously. You can lose money through this platform if you're not accurate in your estimates or you're sloppy with your profit margin calculations.

Not doing enough research: Another tip that many Amazon FBA users miss is that they don't do research on the Amazon site itself before deciding which products they're going to sell. Even if you enjoy fishing, this does not necessarily mean that selling fishing poles on Amazon is a decision that is going to lead to profits. Look at what's selling the most frequently on Amazon, and take note of any markets that may look like they're being underrepresented.

Having too many similar products: Unlike the notion of a niche website that we've already discussed, you do not have to worry about keeping a product line that is similar when you're using Amazon FBA. Because your seller profile is not going to define the type of business that you're running, you have the freedom to pick and choose the products that you want to sell. This can be great for someone who is good at doing research on products within Amazon's website. By figuring out the profit margin that's possible from certain products that are on the market, you should be able to make better financial decisions for yourself and your business.

Chapter 22 Frequently Asked Questions

What does Fulfillment by Amazon represent?

Fulfillment by Amazon (FBA) is a very interesting option provided by this platform, which can help merchants boost their business by taking advantage of Amazon's expertise and resources, fast, free and trustworthy shipment, and outstanding customer support services. By choosing this option, you can send your inventory to the platform's warehouses (fulfillment centers) so that they can be stored over there and then leave everything to Amazon, including the picking, packing, and shipping of your customers' orders.

FBA is eligible for all the product categories and subcategories showing up on the Amazon Seller account. It is also available for any reseller who is curious to try it. The maximum weight limit for this program is 30 kilograms per product, so this is a requirement you need to know right from the start. You can test how your products are selling on Amazon, as well as send plenty of them to the fulfillment centers because you don't have to pay for anything upfront. You merely have to spend on their services that you use at the end of the month or when you make a sale.

What exactly is the Amazon Seller Central?

When selecting the selling plan, you should be able to see the prices of both plans easily. The Individual account costs $0.99, while the Professional one amounts to $39.99. These are both monthly fees, and you are charged 30 days after the registration process.

Is it possible to create an Amazon Selling account for free?

Unfortunately, this is not an option on this platform because you need to choose between an Individual or Professional account.

What do I have to do in order to comply with Amazon's return policy?

Amazon will ask you to provide the following methods for returns:

- a return address;
- a prepaid return level; and
- a full refund without asking for the product to be returned.

How do consumers recognize the Fulfillment by Amazon products on the platform?

These products have the "Fulfillment by Amazon" logo, which provides the customers with the information that support service, returns, packing, and delivery are handled by Amazon.

How to label individual products?

When you wish to add your listings on the platform, you will be faced with a decision that can influence your further success on Amazon. To be precise, you have to select the labelling option, whether you want to send the products using EAN or UPC barcodes (these products fall into the Commingled Inventory or Stickerless category), or label the products properly (Labeled Inventory) to hide the original barcode completely. Commingled Inventory can be combined with other inventories from different merchants; that's why your customers might get products from different resellers, which may or may not have the same features as yours. Amazon will not open the boxes to check which product is the right one and from which merchant it has come from to ensure the authenticity of the merchandise. The Stickerless option, on the other hand, only refers to the products, not to the delivery. Although it may be a bit time-consuming and complicated, you may need to label the items well to protect your inventory and make sure that your customers are getting what they have ordered.

How to print labels for your own products?

When you are adding new products (inventory) from your Seller Central account (you will need to go into "Inventory Amazon Fulfils" and then "Send/replenish inventory") or just preparing an inventory, you are entering something called "shipping workflow." It will provide extra guidance on how to prepare your inventory to be shipped to Amazon's warehouses, thus giving you the option to customize the shipment considering the selections that you make during each step. At one point, you will be prompted to choose the labelling option and allow you to print your unit labels from the shipping workflow directly. These tags will include details like the product title, which can prove to be very helpful when it comes to matching the label with the right product. You need a printer and blank adhesive papers to print such labels, which can be found on the Amazon website or any store that sells office supplies.

Is there a possibility for Amazon to add the labels on your products?

This is a possible option, especially when you are entering the shipping workflow guide. You can simply select Amazon Label Service when prompted with the labelling options. This is a valid solution if you find the private label process too complicated and time-consuming.

How to pack products when sending them to Amazon?

You can find two different types of packing products before sending them to Amazon's warehouses below.

- Individually packed goods means that every box contains one or few units, depending on conditions and quantities.
- Packing items in a case is an option that will allow the merchant to place the products with the same SKU and condition into one box. The boxes will have the same quantity and the same item in them. When Amazon receives these boxes, they will only scan one item from the box and place the whole thing in your inventory. Amazon does not need to scan all the items, considering they are all the same.

When the reseller sends the products to Amazon, they can only be sent using one type of packing per shipment. Although they will be added to the inventory, if the merchant has individually packed items and cases with packed items, he or she will need to send them separately to Amazon.

How to choose a shipping method and carrier to send your inventory to Amazon?

The starting point of creating a new shipment is the "Send/replenish inventory" tab, which is present in the "Inventory Amazon Fulfils" section of your account. It is also possible when you have a work-in-progress inventory and you use the "shipping workflow" tool. By using the latter, you will receive step-by-step instructions on how to prepare your merchandise to be sent over to Amazon, including details about customizing your shipment according to the selections that you make at each step. One of them will allow you to choose from the shipping methods below:

- Small Parcel Deliveries (SPDs) represent individually packed and labelled products (one product per box), all prepared to be shipped.
- Less-Than-Truckload (LTL) shipments are, in fact, a mixed delivery because it contains pallets and individually boxed products. In this case, some of the products may be sent to different destinations, different warehouses.
- Full Truckload (FTL) also combines full pallets and individually packed products. The difference, however, is that the whole merchandise is going to one warehouse.

The FBA terms and conditions apply to all products that you send to and are meant to be sold on Amazon, regardless of the shipping method that you select. You can find more details related to how the platform receives and routes your products if you check these terms and conditions.

You can also choose a different carrier, other than the one provided by Amazon. Costs can be higher in this case, but if you do want to go ahead with this option, you will need to work with a trusted carrier that is capable of providing you with valuable information like a valid tracking number for SPD, the pro/freight bill number for FTL or LTL deliveries, and the bill of lading (BOL).

You can't send the inventory to Amazon using a privately-owned car, however. It can only be done by a registered carrier.

How to create shipping labels?

The shipping workflow is a sequence and tool where you can simply choose the type of labels that you want to have (if there is any). When selecting Small Parcel Delivery (SPD), you will be prompted to print shipping labels (just one per box) and packing slips. You will also need to place the packing slip inside the box, on the top side, so that it can be seen immediately after being opened at the Amazon's warehouse. The information that you should include are the destination and return addresses, while the label should be positioned just outside the sealed box as an addition to labels added by the carrier.

If you select Less-Than-Truckload, you still need to print a label per each box, which has to be placed outside of it so it can be seen when unwrapping the pallet. On the pallets, the tags have to be placed in a top-center position on each side (on the stretched wrap).

Adhesive labels can be found at any office supplies store or on Amazon.

Is it possible to arrange a shipment of inventory directly from an overseas supplier?

This is not an acceptable option because Amazon can't be used as the final address, importer or consignee when sending products from overseas. In this case, merchants will have to make the necessary arrangement to import and clear the shipment of customs. Only after doing this that they can send the inventory to Amazon's warehouses.

How to notify Amazon in advance regarding the products that I'm sending to them?

You have three options of sending products over to Amazon: Small Parcel Delivery (SPD), Less-Than-Truckload (LTL), and Full Truckload (FTL). For the last two choices, you will need to arrange delivery appointments; otherwise, the fulfillment centers may decline your shipment. In order to arrange a delivery appointment with the warehouse where you want to send the inventory, you will need first to download the Fulfillment by Amazon booking form, fill it, and email it to the carrier. In this form, you will have to place the ZIP code (you can find it in the Shipping Queue section of your account). Once the carrier has received your form, they will send it to the Amazon's Fulfillment Center to schedule the best delivery timing. It usually takes around 24 hours for the warehouse to reply back to the carrier with a confirmation for the delivery time.

Conclusion

After reading through this guide, you should feel informed and ready to get started embarking on the journey of FBA business ownership. The benefits are obvious and the potential for profit is enormous if you are willing to put in the strategic work and effort. Many people have invested the time and turned Amazon into their main source of income – now you can too.

It starts off simply: creating your account and arming yourself with the tools of the trade. With the right apps, you can figure out the best way to get a bang for your buck. You'll become an expert at the practice of buying low and selling high, especially with the help of the tools that software developers are continually improving.

Once you've built up your inventory of items you sought out with expertise for their appropriate ranking and adherence to Amazon restrictions and guidelines, you are ready to start a shipment. The packing materials are costly, but remember that you will be able to deduct the cost from your income at the end of the tax season. When you create a shipment with your Amazon Seller account, you will receive detailed instructions on how to pack your shipment and where to send it.

When you've sent your first shipment, be aware of the selling and storage fees that will be levied against you. The advantages of being a professional seller are numerous, but particularly with regard to these selling fees, since you won't pay extra for every item. Use the FBA revenue calculator, another tool in your toolbox, to determine the potential earnings from your sale.

If you feel comfortable with retail arbitrage but are seeking to take it to the next level, or if you are entering Amazon FBA with previous experience selling online, private labeling is for you. Buying inventory cheaply and marketing it under your personal brand is a way to ramp up your earnings. The competition is fierce, but if you choose your products wisely, it can have huge rewards. Even with the right product choice, you will still need to do the most to market your business and get the coveted Buy Box benefits.

A lot of marketing is just common sense: you need to have an attractive sales page so your products present well. There are tricks of the trade, however, that will improve your standing. Offering discounts can help get you the necessary exposure to generate reviews, and taking advantage of Amazon's advertising function with the help of keyword-finding aids will improve your chances – as long as you know how to properly invest in your campaigns.

The technical side of things can get complicated, but this guide should help you feel more comfortable in the awareness of the potential pitfalls that lie ahead. Amazon businesses are rewarding, but you need to be properly equipped with the right legal knowledge in order to avoid the consequences of a mismanaged business.

Once you get started with Amazon FBA, you may find yourself encountering unique issues that aren't addressed in this guide. For those situations, you can address your inquiry to the online community of the FBA Sellers through Seller Central or on other communities like Reddit. There forums offer a framework for the exchange of novel ideas that could revolutionize your selling. Be open to the suggestions of others, as they could help you get ahead of the game.

Lastly, never fail to remember the importance of investing in yourself, for yourself. With Amazon FBA, you are in control. This means you have to be capable of motivating yourself to make the most of this opportunity. The more work you are willing to put into FBA, the more you will get out of it, but only if you are willing to go the distance. It may be called passive income, but you have to actively strive to reach that point. The time you don't spend going after your share of the market is time you leave to other people to take it from you. After reading this book, the next step is to go register as an FBA seller. Armed with this knowledge, the success is yours for the taking.

AMAZON FBA

AMAZON FBA: HOW TO BUILD A SUCCESSFUL E-COMMERCE BUSINESS SELLING ON AMAZON. ACHIEVE YOUR FINANCIAL FREEDOM ONLINE NOW WITH THIS STEP-BY-STEP GUIDE FOR BEGINNERS.

Description

Amazon FBA is an incredible business model that has the capacity to allow everyday people to get into a profitable home-based business for relatively cheap. Due to the improved services being made available by both Amazon and suppliers like Alibaba, getting involved in a business like this is easier than ever before.

Depending on how you want to run your business, you can be as hands-off or hands-on as you want with Amazon FBA. You can choose to have Amazon completely run everything by having them manage fulfillment and paying them to manage your advertisements if you wanted. In this case, all you would have to do is purchase products and upload your product descriptions, as well as manage your advertisements. Or, if you wanted to be more hands-on, you could take advantage of all of these features and run your own organic promotional efforts through social media. There truly is no limit on how you can run your business and how involved or passive it can be.

One of the greatest things about Amazon FBA is that it is a business that you can start on the side of whatever else you are doing in your life. Because so much of the heavy lifting is being done by Amazon, you can begin your business while you are still working full-time elsewhere or even while you are running your own business completely separate of your Amazon FBA business. The versatility here is incredible and offers the opportunity for many people to shift their income from being primarily linear or earned from a job to being primarily online or earned through Amazon FBA. Many people even quit their jobs and other businesses entirely as they earn $10,000+ per month through Amazon FBA, which results in them not truly having to do anything else anyway.

This guide will focus on the following:

- How to find profitable products to sell
- Ordering product from suppliers
- Shipping
- Creating your own amazon seller central account
- Creating your brand
- Creating your product listing
- Selling fees
- Amazon FBA seller pricing and repricing tools
- Driving traffic to your product
- Scaling your amazon FBA business
- Tips for success... AND MORE!!!

Introduction

Living paycheck to paycheck, truth be told, is no way to live at all. From a financial standpoint, it is neither suitable nor sustainable and the stress of worrying about your money running out before the end of the month is going to eventually get to you. Far too many variables involved can quickly cause you to hit rock bottom financially if you do not have any savings, an emergency fund, or something to fall back on if things took a turn for the worse tomorrow and you happen to find yourself out of a job. Yikes!

Thankfully, though, it is not all doom and gloom, since the digital age that we live in has afforded us plenty of opportunities to bounce back, generate a passive income stream and start an online business in half the time it normally take, thanks to E-Commerce platforms like Dropshipping, eBay and Amazon FBA.

Amazon FBA Explained

Online shopping, a concept unheard several decades ago, has emerged to become a part of life for the average consumer. Statistics from 2017 alone, state that more than 1.66 billion shoppers made purchases online and, within that same year, online retail sales globally accounted for almost $2.3 trillion. That number is expected to double by the time 2021 rolls around. An unstoppable force, the online retail space is set to grow bigger and better over the next few years. It is already showing signs of becoming the preferred shopping method for consumers. It is fast, easy, convenient, safe and they do not even have to leave the comfort of their own homes to get the items they need. No more long commutes, sitting through traffic and battling long queues at the stores just to get what they want. Now their products come directly to them with minimal effort. No wonder online retail is so popular, servicing everything from masses to niche markets and more.

Since Jeff Bezos founded it, Amazon has experienced growth at a rapid rate. It is now responsible for 80% of all retail growth that takes place online in the United States *alone*. By the end of 2019, the e-retail giant is estimated to hold 53.7% of the total sales made online in the U.S. and that is going to amount roughly $325 billion in sales. That is impressive by any standards and with more people turning to Amazon to everything from their daily essentials to niche products you can online get online, this is going to be every seller's passive income dream come true.

There are many ways for a seller to get their goods moving online, but FBA is still one of the most profitable and popular methods by far. As one of today's most lucrative methods of earning an online income, Amazon FBA has quickly become the preferred E-Commerce solution, especially for those who have been selling their products on eBay for a while. Managing an online business has never been easier since Amazon FBA was introduced, with the platform helping you out by overseeing all the nitty-gritty details so you can focus on the thing that matters most: *Running your business.* The platform has even made its tagline *"You sell it, we ship it"* to show just how easy it can be to run a business, even if you are a beginner.

FBA stands for *Fulfilment by Amazon* and it is currently home to more than 2 million people, counting worldwide, who are using this platform to market and sell their goods. It could be goods that you are selling wholesale or in bulk, goods that you made yourself, even pre-loved items that you no longer want can still bring in some money so nothing goes to waste. As the name "FBA" implies, you sell your products through the platform and Amazon does the shipping for you. Here is a swift brief of how the complete process works:

- You send your goods to Amazon and they store it in their warehouses.

- A customer browses Amazon's website and when they like what they see, they purchase your product.

- Amazon picks up the products, packs it and ships it to the customer using the order details received.

- Amazon helps you keep track of your order until it safely arrives on the customer's doorstep

- You have one happy customer.

- If there is a problem with the order, Amazon steps right in and handles any returns or refunds on your behalf.

Picture 1

Easy, right? Almost as if the hardest part of your job is going to be procuring the goods. FBA is doing so well that half of the platform's sales are originating directly from third-party sellers, all of which are using FBA to get the job done. Once you have enrolled in Amazon's FBA program, you will be able to reap the benefits and perks that its other members are already enjoying too. Like automating your order fulfillment for example. Easily done by taking advantage of Amazon's advanced shipping and fulfillment services. You will be able to earn more sales when you become part of Amazon's Prime customer tier.

Chapter 1 How to Find Profitable Products to Sell

The question of how to find profitable products to sell is one that depends heavily upon your preferred method of acquiring inventory. If you already have experience selling online and have the funds necessary to invest in your own line of products, head to the Private Labeling section for an in-depth description of the process.

If this is your first time venturing into online sales and you are looking for a quick easy way to get some experience selling and make a sizable supplementary profit, retail arbitrage is the name of the game.

After you've gotten comfortable using the scanner, it is time to hit the streets looking for those discounted and clearance items. The most important thing to address here is to find products for sale at a discount. At the same time, the product also needs to be able to sell. If it doesn't sell quickly enough, it will sit in the warehouses racking up fees. So, how do you know if an item will sell well?

Amazon Ranking System

Amazon uses its own raking system to categorize the products on its website. By looking at this ranking system, you can figure out how well an item sells. Items with lower numbers sell more quickly, which means more of them are bought on a daily basis. An item's ranking in included in the product description.

The Amazon Ranking System is important to understanding how the business of FBA works. First of all, know that a product's rank is based on its sales. It does not take into account reviews or ratings. This is not to say reviews and ratings are not useful; they can be encouraging for people to buy your items, which is how they ultimately contribute to the ranking a product earns. Sales are evaluated relative to other products in a category, so the ranking is not about the quantity of items sold.

Ranking plays an important role for all products sold on Amazon, but particularly for books, it becomes crucial to be aware of the item rank. If you are not selling books, it is important for different reasons. If you are looking at a product ranking for retail arbitrage, you are aiming for an item with a rank lower than 50,000 in its category. For private label, 12,000 is a better goal. The problem with sales rankings is that they cannot tell you everything about how an item will sell. They change over time and are based on the most recent sale period, so they are not necessarily reflective of an item's overall selling potential.

When you are looking to sell an item, you want to be sure that is desirable for the customer, but also that the competition is not too stiff to break into. To better get a sense of the accuracy of the sales rank, check out the reviews it has. If an item has many reviews and a good rank, you know that its rank is a result of sustained performance and not just a temporary jump.

If you are concerned about the rank of the product you are selling, refer to the section of this guide on Amazon Pay-Per-click (PPC) advertising, a sure-fire way to improve the visibility, and thus selling potential, of your product.

Amazon Guidelines

There are some products that cannot be sold through Amazon FBA. Counterfeit products are not allowed. You can check Amazon's restricted product list to figure out which items are disallowed by Amazon; some are not completely disallowed, but restrictions are placed upon them. A few examples from the list of restricted products include: alcohol, food and beverage, tobacco and drug paraphernalia, weaponry, make-up and skin care items, medical products, animals, electronics, services, and art. For a complete and up-to-date list with specific information on restrictions, it is advisable to visit Amazon's official website for more information.

If you are interested in getting approval for items that are restricted to sell on Amazon (for example, beauty products or foodstuffs), you will need to register with a professional account. Then, you will need to seek approval by submitting no less than 3 paper invoices from authorized wholesale suppliers in reasonable quantities (at least 200 units). Retail arbitrage will not work for getting approval to sell unauthorized products; you will need an established business.

Chapter 2 Selecting the Right Product to Sell

How Can You Find the Right Product to Sell on Amazon?

Finding the right product to sell on Amazon may not be the most straightforward task, considering selling something that you like may already be sold by others. After all, you are in this game for the profit. To achieve your objectives, you may need to go the extra mile to discover the hidden secrets of selling on this global platform.

The ideal product to be sold on Amazon needs to have high demand associated with low competition to ensure that it isn't sold by many merchants. This is common sense since your goal is to find a niche that meets such a requirement. Having your private label can be a considerable advantage in this case, too, because you can mark your place in the market. You can then go after the potential customers without being bothered by competitors.

In this chapter, you can find all the necessary details related to products, which can get jaw-dropping high profits, how to conduct market research, how to test your competition, and which bestseller categories are on Amazon. When hundreds of millions of products are being sold on this platform, choosing the right goods to advertise can prove to be a challenging task. That's why you have to know exactly what you are looking for in the Amazon catalogue. By respecting the general guidelines, you can also find the best products to sell.

How to Recognize a Good Product?

What is the ideal product to sell on Amazon? How does it look like? What are the main characteristics you need to consider when choosing a merchandise? These are only a few questions to ask yourself at the beginning of this process. Regarding the latest question, you can find some key information on how to recognize the best product.

Affordable retail price, usually between $25 and $50

According to recent studies, this price range is big enough to cover fees on Amazon related to storage, fulfillment, and advertising. This is when you have high sales, and the volume of sales can easily cover all these expenses and guarantee a handsome profit. If the price is above $50, then many of the customers will no longer consider its attractiveness, and the rate of the goods is what people see. Hence, the purchases will drop significantly.

Very low seasonality

Meaning, the ideal outcome is not influenced by season fluctuation of sales. You need a product that can generate profits throughout the whole year, not just during a specific season.

Lesser reviews for the top sellers

Usually, 200 is good value in this case. However, less than 100 would be even better.

Room for improvement

You can analyze the feedback received from the customers and improve your product based on them.

Easy manufacturing

Such a product has to be easily manufactured and made of resistant materials; thus, you probably need to avoid glass. You also have to keep it simple. So, electronics and sophisticated goods are some examples of the things you should avoid.

Of course, these are just guidelines since your ideal product may be different from the other merchants. It's all about knowing exactly what to sell in the niche you choose to conduct your business.

Finding Products Fast and Easy

By this moment, you know what to look for in the massive database of the Amazon platform. However, you will need some proper tools to help you in this challenging mission. You need to find measurable information related to products, such as demand, price, seasonality, sales, rating, dimensions, price, and many more.

The Jungle Scout Web App can come in handy to help you scan the products from the platform using the Product Database extension. Another exciting feature is the Product Tracker, which can enable you to track inventory, sales activity, rankings, and prices over some time.

To make up your mind regarding the products to sell on Amazon, you need to track them for a few weeks before deciding after viewing the report provided by the Product Tracker feature. By doing so, you can get a clear idea about how the product performs. If you want to find a suitable niche with a high demand, a handy tool can be the Niche Hunter feature of the Jungle Scout Web App. This extension analyzes the most frequent keywords to discover in-demand goods. It can display a list with plenty of products that buyers search for as well. Furthermore, the feature provides an Opportunity Score, which is based on a search algorithm called Listing Quality Score (LQS). It is responsible for identifying the products with high demand and extremely low listing. The higher the Opportunity Score is, the better.

The Jungle Scout Web App can also be used with the Google Chrome extension to test a multitude of keywords. This process can also display some impressive results from which you can easily find out the competition levels for many products. Using all these tools, you can come up with a list of 20 products which fit all of your requirements, but these products will have to be tested.

Comprehensive Market Research

Once you made up your mind regarding the products you want to sell, the first question you need to ask yourself is: "How many items can I sell during a month?" The goods which have to be filtered by this query have to respect the following requirements.

Proper Sales Distribution

Meaning, one or two merchants do not dominate the niche market. Instead, the sales are distributed amongst a few sellers

Satisfactory Demand

Satisfactory demand is considered when the most active sellers on this market can easily sell at least ten items per day.

If you can generate ten sales per day or 300 per month, that's an outstanding figure to start with on Amazon. Jungle Scout extension can help you with this research since it can easily display a report after typing a few relevant keywords. Aside from the top merchandisers, it will also inform you of their sales volume, product prices, item demand, and many more.

Test Your Competition

After you have shortlisted the products that you want to sell, the second question to ask is: "What is the competition selling this item for?" Again, the Jungle Scout app can come in handy since it can show you some fascinating information like reviews and score ratings. The reviews are the most important aspect think about when analyzing your competitors since the number can give you a distinct idea about the size of the competition. A high number of review indicates a very competitive market - the kind of category you have to stay away from.

Moreover, the tool can also show you a list of products on demand that have a small number of reviews. This information is pure gold because that is what you need to get into. Excellent opportunities are usually referred to highly demanded products with less than 200 reviews; when we're talking about less than 100 studies, these are unique chances. To do your homework properly when assessing competition, you may need to read its reviews to improve your products before selling them as well. Furthermore, you can use the Jungle Scout app to establish which items will be your secondary products. These are the goods that you can still get some profits out of, but you may need to track the results for at least a week or two. By doing so, you are already one step ahead of your competitors.

Also, when studying your competition, it matters to think about a significant feature: Amazon Best Seller Ranking. To explain this term simply, it refers to the order the products that are being listed on a page. The platform sorts and arranges every merchandise that was sold at least once into a hierarchy, which is the Best Seller Ranking (BSR). Using this indicator and the Jungle Scout sales estimator tool you can roughly calculate the product sales volume of your competitors. To be specific, you can choose the category, the marketplace, enter the BSR, and obtain their sales estimation. Such a tool can provide you with the right information to become one step in front of your competition once you apply the proper strategies and get the expected results. If the items that you are selling only have a few reviews, you can seriously play a significant role in this market niche after making some sales.

To be successful on Amazon, you will need to sell the right products. To make that happen, you have to be extremely practical and sell what is in high demand and has high chances to be sold. It does not necessarily have to be what you like because there may be plenty of other merchants desiring the same product. Furthermore, you might face a steep competition with more established sellers if you insist on doing so. You also have to be incredibly passionate about the products you are selling because you need to know everything about every merchandise to provide the information that the customers need to see, as well as to improve its quality. That is one way for you to create a well-appreciated brand, which the consumers will want to trust and buy from again.

Best Selling Categories on Amazon

One good starting point to select the right products to sell on this platform is to check the statistics of the bestselling categories and sub-categories. The good news is that it's the kind of information that can readily be found on the Amazon website. Therefore, you can browse through the site's categories and wait for each one to display the best sellers. If you limit your search on the specific sections, you will find the best-selling merchants, who may also be extremely competitive; that's why tackling them may not be the wisest thing to do.

However, if you go further and browse through the sub-categories, you may come across best sellers that are worth your efforts. Some products are merely better sold under a private brand, but the areas that may be for everyone are:

- kitchen and dining
- pet supplies
- sports and outdoors
- patio, lawn, and garden
- home and kitchen

Chapter 3 Ordering Product from Suppliers

You now have a list filled with excellent possibilities for products that you could be selling in your shop, which means that you are ready to start sourcing these products so that you can move on to actually selling them! Ordering products tend to be the most daunting part of the entire business, as this is the part where you are taking the biggest risk in your Amazon FBA business. When it comes to ordering products, you are now relying on the idea that these products are going to sell out and you are going to earn a profit from them have sold. If it did not work out in your favor, you could be out a large amount of money and in possession of many products that you do not want to have any longer.

This means that at least some of the stress should be taken off and that you can start settling into the idea that you are going to be successful, because you are using a winning guideline for how you can earn money using Amazon FBA.

In this chapter, you are going to go through important series of finding suppliers and qualifying them for your business. You are also going to learn about how you can place your order, and when it is the right time to pull the trigger on placing your order. This way, you can feel confident that you have ordered your products properly and at the right time.

Selecting Possible Suppliers for Amazon FBA

The first thing that you need to do is create a list of possible suppliers that you might consider for stocking your Amazon

FBA shop with. At this point, you can easily begin to identify possible suppliers by doing a Google search on suppliers who offer a particular product that you are looking for. When it comes to looking for suppliers you want to look at both wholesalers and manufacturers, as both are going to be able to offer the services that you need to stock your Amazon FBA shop. Avoid shopping through other retailers as their markups are going to be excessive for this particular purpose, since their products are priced for consumers and not businesses who want to purchase large quantities.

As you look for suppliers, be sure to jot down possible suppliers next to every single product that you are considering selling in your store. This way, you can have access to their information for reference when you begin to qualify the suppliers, which will make it easier for you to compare them against one another and validate their quality. Ideally, you want to have 2-3 suppliers per product variety to ensure that you are going to have plenty to choose from. If you have only one, you can still jot it down, but it may not measure up during the qualifying process, which means that you may have a lower chance of stocking that particular item unless your possible supplier is high quality.

After you have found all of the possible suppliers who can help you stock your shop, you want to start writing down important information about each supplier. Think of all of the information that would be relevant to you purchasing their products, and use that to help you create comparison charts. You want to consider how expensive their products are, what their minimum order quantity is, how expensive shipping is, how long it takes for their products to arrive after being shipped, and how they handle quality control complaints. You also want to consider where they are located, as this might contribute to how easy or difficult they are to communicate with. If a company is located overseas, it may indicate that they will be more challenging to communicate with due to the language and cultural barriers that you both face. That being said, overseas companies do tend to produce cheaper goods, so consider the quality of the written content on their website to identify how easy they are to interpret. If their written content is incredibly low or poorly translated, it may indicate that they are going to be harder to communicate with and that you might run into troubles with communication. If their written content seems easy to interpret and well written, chances are they will be easier to communicate with which will make your job easier when you choose to work with them.

With your comparison charts completed, take a moment to disqualify obvious non-contenders. This means any company who is going to be too expensive to shop through, any company with low-quality shipping services, or any company who might be too challenging to communicate with should be disqualified. At this point, there is no reason to further research these particular companies as possible suppliers, if you can already tell that they are not offering what you are looking for.

Qualifying Suppliers and Their Products

Any suppliers that have made it past the obvious disqualifications on your comparison charts are now ready to enter the qualifying stage. This is where you are going to qualify both suppliers and their products to determine which company is going to offer the highest quality of products and services for what you are looking for. This part of the process can be lengthy as you are going to be researching and testing several different companies to ensure that the products that you are going to be stocking are high quality and are coming from great suppliers.

The first step in qualifying a supplier is to make contact with them. As you make contact with the supplier, message them to let them know that you are interested in considering their products for your shop. You can also ask questions such as how long shipping typically takes, what shipping methods they use, how early you should order products when you need to restock, and what their minimum quantity orders are. Even if these types of questions are already answered on the website, make sure to ask them in the email as well. In doing so, you gain the opportunity to see how well they communicate and whether or not they offer positive service when you are inquiring about doing business with them. At this point, some suppliers might take a long time answering, or they might answer in a way that is difficult to understand or that suggests that there will be great difficulty in overcoming language or cultural barriers when you are purchasing with them. This does not mean that they are a bad supplier, but it does mean that you might have difficulty communicating with them to deal with any possible needs or issues that you may face along the way.

Once you have received information back from a possible supplier and you have scored the quality of service and communication that they have offered, you want to move on to ordering samples from them. Ideally, you should order one sample of every single product that you are considering buying from them, so that you can get a hands-on feel for the quality of that product. This is your primary opportunity to engage in quality control on the physical products that you are considering selling, so it is incredibly important. Do not rely on reviews and probability here: *always test the product.* If you do not, you might risk having a low-quality product for sale that could do great damage to your reputation as well as cost you significantly in returned orders or inability to move product. *Do not skip this step.*

At this point, you have effectively established a personal opinion on suppliers and you have validated the quality of their products. The last step before committing to a supplier is doing additional research to see what you can learn about that supplier. Remember: sometimes, salespeople will do and say; everything they need to in order to get you to purchase from them, but then the quality of service goes downhill from there. This does not mean that everyone will do this, but some businesses are guilty of it and if you are caught in this, it can leave you in a huge deficit with your products. The best way to avoid this is to look for external evidence that the supplier you have chosen is going to be able to offer high-quality products and service. You can do this by looking for external reviews on their company, which can be done by either Googling their company for reviews, or by joining social media groups and online forums devoted to e-commerce. In these areas, you can find reviews by real people who have actually worked with that particular company to see what the truth is about that particular company. This way, you can identify any possible issues beforehand in order to avoid being caught in an unwanted situation with expensive products on hand.

When and How to Place Your Order

You should now feel confident in who are planning to order your products from, and which products you are going to be stocking your store with for your launch. Now, you need to know how to determine when you should place your order and what needs to happen for your order to be placed. When it comes to Amazon FBA, the way that orders are placed are slightly different and do require more steps, so be sure to pay close attention to this part to ensure that you are following the steps correctly. Doing this incorrectly could lead to an expensive mistake where Amazon ships your products back to the supplier because they were not properly registered, which you would then have to pay for. You would also have to pay again for your products to be shipped back to Amazon, which could result in three possible charges as opposed to one, which can be incredibly expensive on large shipments of stock.

The first thing you need to understand is that you do not have to order your products right away. In fact, you should not order your products just yet, as you will want to have some form of brand and audience in place before you begin launching products, therefore you have people to market your products to. So, until you begin engaging in organic social media marketing and building a small name for your brand, do not order products just yet. This proactive marketing is a crucial first step for E-Commerce businesses as this is how you establish your earliest crowd and begin to guarantee your earliest success. Ideally, you should have 500-1,000 people in your social media audience on your chosen primary platform before you begin to actually release products to anyone. This way, you have a strong, healthy audience filled with people who have already shown interest in the types of products that you are going to have available.

After you have an existing audience to launch to, you can submit your orders for your chosen products and start having them shipped to Amazon's warehouse. This way, you have your products ready to go for the launch date and you officially move your project into motion. At this point, you are making your launch a real thing and you are reaching the point of no return.

With ordering your products, you are going to have to fulfill your supplier's requirements and fulfill Amazon's requirements in order to purchase your products, and have them shipped to and accepted by Amazon's employees. You should start by approving your products in the Amazon backend, so that when you order your products from the manufacturer Amazon already approves them.

You can have your products approved on Amazon by signing into your Amazon Seller Central account and going to "Manage Inventory." There, you want to select "New Inventory" and then fill out all of the details about the new products that you are going to be stocking that will be sent to Amazon. What information is needed will depend on what types of products you are sending, so the best guidance to follow here is everything that you see on screen. Make sure that everything Amazon requests are filled out to the best of your ability. Be especially careful in uploading product SKUs into your product profile, as Amazon will deny any products that do not have the exact SKU that you have uploaded so despite tiny inaccuracy can turn out to be disastrous.

After you have registered your new product into your Amazon Seller Central account, you can go to your Manage Inventory page once again, highlight the chosen product, and click "Action on Selected" and then click "Send/Replenish Inventory." You will then be prompted to create a new shipping plan for the product that you are going to be shipping to the Amazon warehouse, so that Amazon's employees know what is happening with your shipment.

The first step in creating your shipping plan is confirming the ship-from address, which is the address of your supplier that will be shipping the products to Amazon. Make sure that you get this address correct because if there are any troubles with your shipment, Amazon is going to send it back to the manufacturer, and if the address is wrong, this could get even more expensive with a lost package.

Next, you need to confirm your packing type. Amazon offers two options to choose from individually packed or case packed. If you are going to be selling individual items, you are going to select individually packed as your packing type. If you are going to be selling multiples grouped together, you want to select case packed. For example, if you were going to sell one individual box of tea, you would select individually packed. However, if you were going to sell ten individual boxes of tea together as a case, you would select case packed. It is worth mentioning that if you are selling individual packages or cases; make sure to mention this to your suppliers so that they can package your products properly for Amazon.

With this information inputted, your basic shipping plan will be designed and now you will have to create the rest of the shipping plan for your package. You will click "Continue to Shipping Plan" and then you will need to select the preparation method. Either you can prepare a shipping plan yourself, or you can request that Amazon creates the shipping plan for you.

Then, you need to prepare and label your products, which will all be done through the systematic system built into Amazon FBA's platform. Next, you will set the quantity and print those labels as needed. Finally, you will preview your shipment, prepare your shipment, choose your shipment type, and then confirm your shipment.

Regarding choosing your shipment type there are two options: Small Parcel Delivery, or Less Than Truckload. Small Parcel Delivery would be anything coming in a single box. For this, you would input the weight and dimensions of each box and put that into your pack list. If you choose Less Than Truckload, this means you are getting a large number of boxes delivered, so you will need to indicate the number of boxes being delivered and enter all of the shipping information from your carrier into them.

Once you have confirmed all of this through Amazon FBA, you can confirm and finalize your order through your supplier. At this point, all you should need to do is purchase the quantity from your supplier and give them Amazon's warehouse address, which can be found in the information with your shipping plan. Then, your products should be shipped to Amazon and they should be managed according to your shipping plans instructions. Information about your shipment will be uploaded directly into your Amazon Seller Central account, where you will be able to see if the shipment has been received and how much stock you have with each product. At first, you should have the entire stock that you ordered, however as it begins to sell you will start seeing those numbers drop.

Chapter 4 Shipping

Now it's time to get your products shipped to their destination! There are a few things you should know right off the bat:

- Always make sure that the cost of customs clearance is included in a freight company's door-to-door service before placing orders overseas.
- Always get a quote in WRITING and make sure that is DDP (delivered duty paid). This means that the seller (not you) has to bear the risks and costs, including duties, taxes and other charges of delivering the goods to it, cleared for importation.
- Ask your supplier for a freight quote. Sometimes they have great relationships and could save you money on your shipments.
- Sometimes it's worth it to send about 20% of your shipment by Air Freight and the remaining 80% by Sea. This way, you don't pay that much more, you get your stock in much faster. This is great to do when:
  o You want to get started sooner; or
  o You're running out of stock, and you must receive it as soon as possible, or you will be out of stock for a long period.
- You must be certain that *all information supplied to the broker, air courier, or postal service is true and correct*. A power of attorney does not extend beyond their role as your Customs Broker. This is one rule you must learn. You are legally responsible for the facts declared in any declaration lodged for clearance purposes. Even if

your broker makes an error, you are legally responsible. One area that few consider in this respect is declared value. It is almost universal practice for Asian suppliers to under-declare the shipment value, or declare the goods as a gift, thinking they are doing you a favor. Chinese suppliers will do it routinely unless at the time of placing the order you firmly tell them not to. The majority of importers insist on them showing false values.
- You don't need to ship the product to you before shipping it to Amazon. We prefer shipping direct. Don't think for a second that your supplier doesn't know that your selling on Amazon and that they can't find your exact listing.

Basics of Shipping

Air shipping vs. Sea

- Air Shipping is usually split into
  - Air Freight – 15-20 days (door to door)
    - More expensive than sea freight
    - Dimensions and weight determine the price
    - Packing type is through cartons or palletized
    - Price will vary more than by sea depending on the period
    - Longer transit times (layovers) is usually cheaper than shorter transit times
- Express – 3 to 5 days (DHL, FedEx, UPS, etc...)
  - Mostly used for samples

- Sea
    - Good for Oversized Products or Bigger Orders
    - Will take 35-45 days
    - Price is determined by dimensions/Volume (CBM – Cubic Meters)
    - Packing type is LCL (Less than Container Load or Consolidation) / FCL (Full Container Load)
        - LCL
            - Best use for below 15cbm shipments
            - You'll share a container with others (sharing the fee)
            - More expensive vs. FCL
        - FCL
            - Different sizes to choose from
            - Safer if all the container goes to the same location

The Larger a product is, the more economical it will be to ship by sea. If it's very small, it may be cheaper to send through Air!

How/When to use Air shipments?

- Launching a new product and you want to get feedback faster (send 30% by air, and 70% by sea can be an option depending on a case by case basis)
- Air shipments are usually better than running out of inventory (a % by air and the rest by sea works as well in this case)

Using Sea shipments

- Extremely cost effective for larger and heavier shipments

- Longer transit time (usually about 40 days from start to end)
    - About 15-20 days from port to port (China to LA) without the customs clearance

Better Management

- If you're shipping products from multiple suppliers, try to consolidate all the products using your freight forwarder. This will improve your margins and save you time managing the shipments.
- Plan and be on the lookout for Chinese holidays
    - Prepare your production accordingly so you can save money on shipping. Shipping during high seasons will cost you more.
- Most of the time, try to avoid DHL, UPS, and FedEx – their cost will be much higher. Use a freight forward or check out the in the "Getting Quotes" section.

Evaluating different freight services for cost-effectiveness

Here I should add a note about cost-effectiveness because it can be too easy to think that the lowest freight cost per item is the one to choose. It may be, but that is not necessarily so.

You should consider what is known as opportunity cost. Faster delivery means a quicker turnover of your capital, and can considerably reduce your capital cost. While I am not teaching business economics, I suggest you consider what it might cost you in lost earnings on the capital needed to pay for your goods while they are in transit. It may cost you interest payments, or it may lose interest that you could otherwise earn.

There is also the need to consider the lost sales and ranking that might result from the delay.

FBA Shipping Labels

Carton Labels

- They are FBA labels applied to the master carton.
- You will receive this label while you're creating your shipment plan in Seller Central.
- Make sure that your Packing Type is "Case-packed products."
- If you're sending in a product with 2 different colors, you'll have to make sure that you don't mix any of the colors. If you fit 25 units in a carton and you're sending 500 units (250 blue and 250 red), you will need to have 10 cartons with 25 units of red and 10 cartons with 25 units of blue.
- Decide WHERE you want those cartons shipped. To your home, warehouse, directly to Amazon?
  - There are pros and cons to all those methods. If you don't ship to Amazon directly, then you're spending more time and money to inspect and ship the products again.
- Those labels are only valid for 3 months. Send them right before the inspection or 1-2 weeks before the final production date.

Inspections

Getting your shipments inspected is a no-brainer. It's not that expensive and it can be the difference between thousands of dollars lost and the quality you were expecting. Is it the last line of defense (if you're shipping directly to

Amazon) before your customers receive the product. You must do it before paying the 70% balance!

Most people don't want to pay for the inspection, here are a few reasons why you must do it:

- It's way cheaper and easier to fix the issue before you paid the remaining 70% balance to your supplier.
- Once you've received the product in EU or US, it's usually too late to do anything about it (in most cases).
- Some suppliers don't want the inspection company to visit their factories (big red flag)
- Freight can be quite expensive, so better make sure that the product is perfect before.
- They will replace the products that don't pass the inspection.

What should they look for?

- The inspection companies know the drill. Nonetheless, you should confirm with them exactly what they'll do before. You'll want them to do:
  - Carton drop test – 5 times at 3 feet high
  - Unit drop test – 2-3 feet high drop
  - Check your competitors' complaints list so that they can test against those key points
  - Verification of quantity, item weight, dimensions, packaging (printing, sturdiness), labels, made in China/PRC marking

Here is a list of the companies that I consider to be reliable:

- Bureau Veritas
- TUV Rheinland

- SGS
- Intertek
- Sinotrust
- KRT Audit Corporation (US based)
- Cotecna
- Topwin (Chinese service cheaper than others)

Getting Quotes

What information you need:

- Carton Size
- # of Cartons
- Gross Weight of shipment or per Carton
- Address of the warehouse where your product is (if shipping FOB)**
- Which port (if shipping FOB)**
- Make sure that the duty rate is included (and is the same in all your quotes so that you can compare them)

**Not necessary if you use to pay your freight through your supplier

I suggest you get a quote for both Sea and Air Freight so that you can compare the difference in pricing. Sometimes you could be surprised. Depending on the weight and size of your product, it will vary a lot.

Where to go to find your Quotes?

- https://www.flexport.com/
- https://freightos.com
- Ask your supplier
- Shop around, they are so many different freight forwarders out there

Both websites above are quite easy to use. You should be able to look at YouTube or directly contact them if you need help.

Inventory Management System

Having a system in place to ensure you don't run out of stock and have too much product on hand is crucial. First, you have to know:

- How many units per day on average you're selling (ASV – Average Sales Velocity)
    - We focus on the last 30 days, but will also look at the last 7 and 14 days to ensure it's still in line.
- You must always be able to answer *"How many days of inventory do I have left?"*
    - Also known as "Days on Hand."
    - It will be easily calculated: (Inventory on Amazon for product X / ASV of product X)
- *When will you need to reorder?* You must know your lead time
    - Lead time = Manufacturing time + Inspection time + Shipping Time
    - Reorder Time = Days on Hand – Lead Time – Safety Margin (14 Days)
    - The Safety Margin is there to minimize the risk of running out of stock
- *How much will you need to order?*
    - During Q4 (November – December will usually be 2-3x your regular ASV!)
        - It varies by category, but it will increase.
    - Reorder Quantity = ASV * 60-90 days
        - We like to order between 60 to 90 days of inventory per order.

- You can also ask your manufacturer to hold onto 30-45 days of inventory in case you need to send in stock faster than you think. This will also save you storage fees.

Chapter 5 Creating Your Own Amazon Seller Central Account

Amazon Seller Central Account Checklist

There are a few details that you will have to provide when creating an Amazon Seller Central account.

Business Information

This field is related to contact information, business name, and address.

Email Address

You have to provide an email address that is suitable for such account. It should be already set up as well because Amazon will contact you immediately through the email.

Credit Card Information

Providing a valid debit or credit card is very important. If you offer details for an invalid one, Amazon will merely cancel your registration. The debit/credit card has to be linked to a valid billing address, too.

Phone Number

Since Amazon will also contact you back by phone during the registration process, you will have to provide a valid phone number you can be reached on.

Tax ID

This particular number is significant during the registration process since you will have to give details like your company's federal TAX ID number (in the US) or the Social

Security Number. During this step, you will be prompted to do the "1099-K Tax Document Interview."

State Tax ID

You will need to mention in which state or states you conduct your business to get the right state tax ID.

For the last two steps of the registration process, it is highly recommendable to consult a tax advisor or different websites like taxjar.com, avalara.com, and taxify.com.

Most Important Questions to Ask Yourself Before Creating an Amazon Seller Central Account

You should not set up the Amazon Seller Account without asking yourself a few questions.

1. Where you will send the Amazon order returns?

As mentioned before, Amazon is a company that's oriented towards customer satisfaction, and they are doing their best to improve the consumer experience on this platform. This also includes handling returns, considering customers can quickly return a product if they don't want it anymore due to different reasons. As a company selling on this platform, you will need to comply with this policy; that's why the return process is something you will need to consider. In other words, you will either need to care of it yourself or outsource it to an agency like tradeport.com or openedboxreturns.com. They specialize in grading and testing returns, as well as in placing the product on sale again.

Also, you have to think of a person from your company who can handle customer inquiries. Know that you not only have to answer everyone but also reply within 24 hours, regardless of the day of the year (according to Amazon's policy). Therefore, all these essential roles have to be figured out already before even creating the Amazon Seller's Account.

2. Is commingling an option if you choose to use Fulfillment by Amazon (FBA)?

The FBA option provides the seller access to a community of customers (Prime members), who spend more money on their Amazon purchases. This group has more than 100,000,000 members worldwide. However, you are not the only merchant who has access to this exclusive buyers club, given the fact that there are other 2,000,000 sellers in total on this platform, and the majority of them have access to the Prime members (Wallace et al, 2019).

Since you have to make sure that your products get to these customers, you can risk to mingle them with other merchants' goods, which may be the counterfeit versions of your items. The inventory is being sent to the fulfillment centers, where they might mix with the inventory of other sellers. A customer might receive a product as well which did not come from you, might be of lower quality, or even counterfeited. Hence, you have to provide serious explanations to the customer. If they file a complaint, you might also be banned from selling on Amazon, all because of a product which wasn't even yours in the first place. It now depends on you to prevent such thing from happening. When creating the Seller Account, it is "stickerless" by default, so you can commingle with other products from different inventories.

Fortunately, Amazon can give you the option of getting a "stickered" account but ensure to change the type of the account before sending the first shipment to the fulfillment centers. At least, this is the recommended way. You can also opt for the "stickered" selection later, but you might be exposing yourself to risks if you have already sent unlabeled inventory to Amazon.

3. Do you intend to use a Doing Business As (DBA) name for your Amazon Seller account?

This platform can allow you to hide your merchant identity from the customers by using a different name on Amazon. This is an option to consider if you don't want brands knowing that you are selling their products online, as well as when the reseller is the brand itself, and they don't want their partners to know that they do direct marketing on this platform.

4. Are your products in a category permitted by Amazon?

This is a crucial aspect as the FBA program doesn't allow all resellers to sell through some categories. E.g., alcoholic drinks, vehicle tires, gift cards, gift certificates and a few other products like pamphlets, sky lanterns or price tags. If you don't dabble in these things, then you're in luck because you can sell a wide variety of products without a hassle. Of course, it's highly recommendable for them to have a higher profit margin, but they should also be sold quickly.

Another fact that requires your attention is your seller catalog on Amazon. It's terrific to have all the goods added to your list within the first 30 days since the opening of your account. This way, you can easily find out if you will have problems with some specific stock keeping units (SKUs) and brands. In case they are inevitable, you may need to change your catalog or close the account, primarily if Amazon is imposing restrictions on the products you are planning to sell.

Must-Have Skills for Amazon Sellers

The Amazon marketplace is comparable to a wild jungle where only the strongest can survive. As a new seller, you have to be aware that there are 2 million other merchants like you on this website, so you have a stiff competition regardless of the products you are selling. To rise above everyone, you need to possess some skills and knowledge to boost your sales and always be in front of the game.

1. Outstanding marketing content to build the best product listings

There are high chances that others already sell the product you are selling on this platform. However, to make sure that your items come first, you will need to work on optimizing the details related to them. Focus on product title and description, bullet points, and generic keywords (for SEO purposes). Also, you should add very clear images, including the lifestyle photo of the product on sale. The main image needs to have a white background and a resolution of at least 500 x 500 pixels, but it's not necessary to place your brand on it.

2. Knowing how well your product is selling and how to prevent running out of stock

If you have a favorite product on Amazon, you need to be aware that you will eventually run out of stock. To avoid this scenario, you need to know how to replenish your inventory. Depending on the products that you usually sell, you can fill it again. If you are keen on selling one-time buys or close-outs, then you may have a tough time to replenish the stock since the products can be difficult to find again.

3. Choosing if you want to sell the same product or diversify

If you're going to trade one product on Amazon alone, you can benefit from some exciting tools like the alert and forecasting tools from Amazon. Alternatively, you may try getting help from the likes of www.forecastly.com.

4. Knowing how to find and deal with the old inventory

The truth is that some of the products may not be very popular and end up being stored for an extended period in the fulfillment centers. Such goods have to be sold on different selling channels to clear up the inventory in the warehouses since you might need to pay extremely high storage fees for them. The good news is that FBA can easily help you identify the old inventory, while the non-FBA programs force the seller to search by SKU to find the stale stock manually.

5. In-depth understanding of every cost

The majority of the sellers on this platform can understand the necessary expenses related to SKU - level profitability, which leads to an overall result - instead of having a clear idea regarding the SKUs that provide the highest profitability and the products that cost to sell on Amazon. Having a detailed cost situation can help the seller comprehend and put together the overhead expenses and acknowledge that those costs have to be integrated into the total amount.

6. Discovering who sells the same SKU on this platform

Without thorough research, you can end up listing your products on Amazon and discovering that there are plenty of other merchants with the same goods later. They will compete against each other to provide the best price for the product, which leads to low profitability or losses. Before creating the account, therefore, it is essential to find out if the products you are planning to sell are already massively sold on this platform, possibly even by Amazon Retail. If so, you will need to list different products on sale. Furthermore, it pays off to study not only your competition thoroughly but also their merchandise. If you are competing against sellers with low prices, you can't expect to have big profits in this niche. Then, you might realize that it may not be the best category to help you make money.

Furthermore, Amazon only charges a fee after the first 30 days of creating the account, so why should you not use that period to set it up properly? You can create the product offers and start selling to activate your sellable inventory, for one. Even if you don't send any listing to Amazon or sell anything, you can still be charged after 30 days because the account is active. In this period, you need to grow your business perspective on this platform. A good method to make it happen is to ask for feedback.

One of the options is to visit websites like feedbackgenius.com, feedbackfive.com, salesbacker.com, et cetera. They are not free of charge, but at least they are not expensive, so they are an investment worth taking. This strategy can show Amazon that the reseller can perform and comply with the platform's performance and customer-oriented policies.

Chapter 6 Creating Your Brand

While your first products are on their way to Amazon, it is a good idea for you to begin creating your brand. As you already know, your brand is key in helping you set yourself apart from other brands that already exist on Amazon. With your brand, you can create familiarity on Amazon itself, as well as on other platforms such as Instagram, Facebook, and Twitter, where you can drive traffic directly to your Amazon store.

If you chose to create private label products, you would want to have your brand already established *before* ordering them so that they are privately labeled with the right branding. For that reason, you should do this step before you officially purchase your products so that you can feel confident that they are going to match your branding.

In this chapter, we are going to explore all of the basics of launching a brand for your Amazon account, including how you can use other platforms to drive traffic to your website. You will also learn about how you can protect your brand to avoid having other Amazon merchants rip your brand off and potentially destroy your reputation and the credibility of your business along the way.

Choose Your Brand Identity

First things first, you need to choose your brand identity. Your brand identity is the identity by which you are going to be recognized, so you need to make sure that you choose one that is attractive and coherent. Your brand identity includes your name, your logo, your font, your colors, and your imagery. All of these factors are relevant in cultivating your brand, so make sure that you pay attention to all of them.

The name of your brand should be something relevant and catchy. It should make sense to your brand so that it is clear as to why you have chosen this name and what it represents. Ideally, your brand name should not be your own name, unless your own name is already popular and well known. Instead, choose a one or two-word brand name that represents what you are selling so that people will immediately recognize it and know who you are once you begin to establish brand familiarity.

Your logo and brand fonts should be the same, as you want to use your brand fonts in your logo. Typically, brands will choose two fonts that they are going to use to represent their brand. The first font is generally the header font that they are using, and the second font is the body font. These two fonts should go nicely together and should have a feel that is relevant to your industry. For example, if you are selling professional office products, you should use clean fonts like Arial or Helvetica. If you are in an elegant industry, choose something like a script header and a simple body font, such as Dancing Script and Arial.

You need to choose a few colors that are also going to represent your brand. Ideally, you should have three to four colors for your brand: one or two primary colors and then two secondary colors. Your colors are going to be used on everything from your labels to your graphics and everywhere else, so make sure they go well together and that they fit into your overall image. They should also be relevant to your industry by providing the right look and feel to your brand, as out-of-place colors can quickly make your brand seem unprofessional or misplaced.

Finally, you want to choose the actual imagery of your brand. Most brands will produce what is called a mood board, which is essentially a collection of graphics that give the feel for what your brand is going to offer. You might have people lying at the beach and sunsets if your brand is for lounging and relaxing, or you might have pictures of minimalism and fresh flowers if you want a minimalist eco-friendly appearance. Create whatever mood board you desire based on the look and feel that you want your brand to have.

Once you have put all of this together, lay it all next to each other to get a feel for what your final brand is going to be. This will give you an idea as to whether or not it works together and if it is going to provide the right look for your company. If you find that it does not perfectly reflect your brand, you are going to want to make a few adjustments to it so that it gives a better and more coherent feel for your customers.

Apply For Brand Registry

After you have created your brand, go on Amazon, and apply for a brand registry. You should do this before you do anything else with your brand as this is going to protect your brand from possible identity theft on Amazon. A brand registry can be applied for by going onto your professional seller account, heading to your settings, and selecting the "Brand Registry" feature.

In order to register your brand, you are going to have to provide the following information to Amazon:

- The name of your brand (it will need to be registered with U.S. Patent and Trademarks first)
- Brand serial number from your USPTO

- The countries where your products are manufactured and distributed by
- Image of your brand name on a product that you will be selling
- Image of your product label
- Image of your product

Although this can take some time, it is worth doing so that you can protect your brand from being stolen by anyone else on Amazon. Remember, Amazon is an international marketplace, so having this added layer of protection is crucial in helping you avoid any unwanted brand identity theft that could take place.

As well, having this brand registration unlocks more branded features for you on Amazon, including the ability to brand your own storefront and product pages as per your brand's appearance. It is well worth the investment!

Brand Your Product Pages

Each time you upload products to your shop, you should be branding those pages. There are three areas of your product page that you want to brand in order to have your brand clearly displayed for your customers to see.

The first part of your product page you want to brand is your title. Your title can have up to 200 characters in it, so do your best to create a full title that features your brand's name, the title of the product, and anything else that someone may search when they are looking for your products.

The second part of your product page that you should brand is your product description. On Amazon's product pages, you can include up to 5 bullet points of information, with each bullet point containing up to 255 characters. Use these bullet points to provide clear information about what benefits people will gain from using the products and any search terms that they may be looking for when they are searching for products like yours. Refrain from making the bullet points spammy by listing search terms without any context, as this may actually reduce your rankings on Amazon's SEO, or search engine returns.

Finally, you want to brand your pictures. Your pictures should clearly display your product with your branded private label. You can also watermark your images with your brand name in the corner or somewhere along the edges, where it will not interrupt your image so that you can brand your product there as well. Each of your pictures should be relevant to your brand by having your brand's color scheme and mood artistically weaved into your picture. For example, if you have a fresh and clean eco-brand, you might photograph your product on a white background next to fresh green plants. If you have a rustic western brand, you might photograph your product on a wood background next to something like a vintage piece of furniture or decoration. Avoid going too crazy with your images; however, as cluttered images or images with too many decorations in them can be distracting and confusing. People may get overwhelmed with what they are looking at and may find themselves looking elsewhere instead of looking at your products because they simply do not know what they are looking at.

Brand Your Product Labels

In addition to branding your store, you also want to brand your product labels. Whenever you can, source products that allow for private labels so that you can label your products with your logo, fonts, and color scheme. Doing so is going to help you create products that are marketing your brand for you as they feature all of this information directly on them. Now, when someone buys your product, they are going to remember the brand it was purchased from, and they can use this information to buy more for themselves or to encourage their friends to buy something from you.

When you brand your product labels, try to stick to generally the same look on all products. Having the same background colors, imagery, and general design on your product labels will ensure that you are keeping your look uniform. This way, you are increasing your chances of having brand recognition because you are producing the same look every time. A great example of this is Coca-Cola. Their brand is represented by an iconic red with their scripted logo. Every time you look at a Coca-Cola product, you immediately know what it is because the branding is uniform and clear every single time.

Brand Your Amazon Storefront

On Amazon, after you register your brand, you are going to have the opportunity to brand your storefront. Your storefront is basically like your web store or your own private webpage on Amazon's platform that displays your products for sale. Branding your storefront is an important part of making it memorable so that people want to see it and pay attention to your products when they land on your page.

You can brand your storefront by choosing how many pages you are going to have displayed on your store, what those pages are, and what categories they revolve around. You want to design your pages and categories in a way that reinforces the image and brand that you have already begun to develop so that when people land on your page, it feels like it truly belongs to your brand. In other words, *it makes sense.*

When you develop your storefront, a branded video on your front page that is about 30 seconds long is actually an incredible way for you to boost your viewership and your recognition. Although this will take more effort and time investment on your end, doing it can have a huge impact on your customers and can support you with increasing your sales numbers.

With your branded storefront, you can choose to have your own URL if you desire so that you can market both on Amazon's platform and off of it. If you really want to set yourself apart from the other brands on Amazon, this is a great feature. However, it is not necessary, so do not feel like you have to do this if you do not want to. You can still make plenty of money with your Amazon FBA platform without your own URL.

Brand Your Amazon Ads

However, it is important for you to know that this is a feature that is available to help you brand your business. Amazon offers three types of ads: sponsored product ads, sponsored brand ads, and sponsored display ads. Taking advantage of sponsored brand ads is a great way to promote your brand and help boost brand recognition so that you are more likely to make sales with your brand on Amazon. As well, sponsored brand ads provide you with the opportunity to show people what your brand is so that they can find your store and discover what products they are interested in, rather than having your individual products being marketed to them.

Brand Your Other Platforms

Once your Amazon brand has been built, brand your other platforms, too. With Amazon, you are not required to use social media to drive traffic to your store. However, it does help. Driving your own traffic to your own store by building a brand on social media and using that brand to funnel people increases your sales because it means you are no longer relying solely on Amazon's algorithm. You certainly do not have to do this, and if you do not want much involvement in this business you should skip this step, but if you really want to grow your store, this is an important step.

If you are on Instagram, Facebook, Twitter, or anywhere else on social media or the internet itself, make sure that you are branding your accounts. Use your logo in your graphics, choose graphics that are relevant to your brand, and create a brand that is going to help you establish recognition. Then, encourage people from your brand to find their way to your platform and purchase your products!

There are plenty of great books about branding on social media, so I highly recommend you grab one and use that as a part of your mindset growth and personal development if this is something you want to do. A book that is specifically designed around this topic will provide you with ample advice on how to brand each account and how to post in a way that accentuates your brand and gets your name out there in a bigger way.

Chapter 7 Creating Your Product Listing

Product Description

Having a well-crafted product description is important for having and optimized listing page. These are the key reason why it is crucial to have a great product description:

- A strong product description will convert shoppers into customers. More customers will create a better sellers rank which will allow your product to rank better organically. This will in turn create more sales without having to pay for ads.

- The product description is the main place to really highlight why your product is better than your competitors. In other words, this is the place to differentiate your product.

- Many other sellers do not fully utilize the product description, so this is where you can step in to capitalize on their laziness.

Product Description Details

There are some specifications of the description that you need to know:

- You are only allowed 2000 characters, not words!

- Basic formatting is possible - this includes basic HTML: bold, paragraph spacing etc.

Product Detail Tips

You should focus on writing your description as a sales letter, including a specific benefits, product guarantees and distinct call-to-actions.

Start with a catchy headline that will be certain to grab your customer's attention. Immediately give them a reason to buy your product rather than a product from a competitor. Really focus on your customer and how your product will benefit them.

Another great tip is to look at the positive and negative reviews of your competitor's products. See what people really like in other products and ensure that these features and benefits are strongly emphasized in your product description. On the other hand, if your product solves issues in other products that people have complained about, be sure to highlight these too.

You don't need focus on including all your keywords in your product description, although you will want to definitely include your top ones as this will help with ranking your product page on Google.

Here is a template to help your create an effective product description:

"Headline

Sub-Headline

Bullet point

Bullet point

Bullet point

Benefits, Features, and Bonuses.

Guarantee and Call-to-Action!"

It can take up to 30 minutes for changes to appear on your Amazon product page.

Headline: Remember the headline needs to be attention grabbing. For example: "The Secret to Getting in Amazing Shape Without Going to the Gym".

Sub-Headline: Should be a strong continuation of the main headline.

Bullet points: This is where you can highlight the main features of your product. Highlight the advantages of your product! You can also include a bonus offer here.

Guarantee: Include strong guarantees as this significantly improves your conversion rate.

Call-to-Action: Tell your customers what to do! Remind them to buy your product now before shopping around.

If you follow this template for making an effective product description, this will really pay off by making your product stand out from your competitor's, and will drastically increase your conversion rate.

Using High Quality Images

In this section I will be covering why it is extremely important to use very high quality images on your product page. High quality images serve the following roles:

Drawing Attention - they grab a shopper's eye which will entice them to click through to your product over a competitor's. This is particularly important for the very first product image.

Stronger conversion rates - having a selection of high quality images gives a strong sense of professionalism and lets the customer really see and 'feel' the product. Needless to say, this really boosts your conversion rate. Having great images is the closest you can bring the customer to actually looking at a product in a physical store.

Product Image Specifications

- You are limited to 9 product images

- Your main image must have a white background - this is Amazon's guidelines

- Your images should be at least 1000 pixels on the longest side - this allows customers to zoom in to your product.

- Product Image Tips.

- Make your first feature image very high resolution.

- Always use the 9 images available for your product.

- Either hire a professional photographer to take your images or use your own or a friends high quality camera.

- You can then have these edited using a freelance website mentioned previously.

- Do not include promotional text or logos on your main product image - this is against Amazon's guidelines.

- Get pictures of your product from all angles.

Overall, when it comes to selecting and uploading your product photos, make sure that your featured product image is superb. This is your best chance to put your product as close as possible to the customer's hands before they purchase it!

Other Details

In this section I will be explaining how to effectively fill in all of the other details in your product listing dashboard.

Search Terms

This is very important, and you can find this in the "Keywords' tab of the product listing dashboard. This is where you can use the keyword research that you did earlier. Simply plug in your top keywords into this section. This will help Amazon determine what customer searches to show your product for, so this is extremely important for getting your product in front of shoppers.

Product Dimensions

This is found in the 'More Details' tab and it is important to fill in as many details as you can. There will also be other fields that are not relevant to your products, but have a look to see what you can possibly fill in.

These details are not as important as your product description, but Amazon does prefer having as much detail as possible about your product which can help them get your product in front of more people.

Checklist of Required Actions

You're almost at the stage to launch your new product! Here is a checklist of actions that you must complete before starting on the next section:

- Conduct keyword research
- Create an effective title

- Highlight the features and benefits of your product in the bullet points section

- Create an amazing product description

- Get 9 very high quality photos for your product page

- Complete as many 'Other Details' in the product listing dashboard as you can

Chapter 8 Selling Fees

As you are sending your items off, be aware of the fees you will incur using the FBA service. Amazon does take a portion of the revenue you generate, but in the grand scheme of things, it usually pays to have this minor bit taken out. FBA fulfillment fees are constantly changing; you will need to keep a vigilant watch of the prices to notice how they fluctuate, usually around the time of the change in financial quarter.

Multi-Channel Fulfillment

The fees you are charged for using the FBA service depends on whether you are using only Amazon Fulfillment or Multi-Channel Fulfillment. Multi-channel fulfillment applies to sellers who are using other venues to sell their products, for example using an Etsy page or their own website. Sellers using Multi-Channel use Amazon as one way of directing traffic flow to their other selling channels. If you are interested in Multi-Channel fulfillment, you can look into this option for your business.

Fee types

Fees are applied to your items based on handling of the order, Pick and Pack, and the weight handling. This is why lightweight items can be particularly advantageous for your business. Fees are also applied differently for Media, Non-Media, and Oversized items. Non-Media items are classified in size tiers and also product type.

If you are selling an item over $300.00 worth in cost, you are able to sell it at no cost in terms of the fees leveraged against it.

FBA Revenue calculator

To learn more and calculate the fees that will be leveraged against your items, Amazon has made the FBA Revenue calculator available to its sellers. You need the following information to calculate the revenue you have the potential to earn on an item.

Item Price – what you plan to charge for the item.

Shipping – Because you are shipping through Amazon, they are taking over the fees, so this cost is assumed to be $0.

Order handling – this is determined by the type of item you are shipping and whether or not a flat rate exists for it.

Pick and pack – refers to the cost of the packaging materials necessary to ship your item to the warehouse. You will need to look at materials requirements established by Amazon for packing, which differ depending on the type of item. If you do not properly pack your items, you will be charged for this once they arrive at the warehouse.

Outbound shipping – with Amazon FBA, this is calculated as a flat rate depending upon the item.

Weight handling – Calculated using the scale specified by Amazon, with a special fee included for certain items, such as TVs.

Monthly storage – Charged by cubic feet of volume, differs monthly.

Inbound shipping – the cost of transporting your items to the Fulfillment center. If the items you are ordering have proper labeling, they can sometimes be sent directly to Amazon. This applies specifically to private label goods. With private label goods, your manufacturer can send the items directly to an Amazon warehouse if they meet Amazon requirements. Otherwise, you are responsible for shipping the goods.

Customer service – With FBA, the cost of customer service is already factored into your professional seller account, so there is no charge here.

Prep service – This applies if you opt for Amazon to fulfill your item prep and it is calculated per item.

Once you have inputted the above values, the Revenue Calculator will tell you the Referral cost and the Variable closing fee.

Storage fees

Amazon charges sellers a fee for storage, which is why it is critical to select items that sell well and quickly. Otherwise, you will be charged for the items that remain in storage. You are charged for the total cubic feet of your items.

The cost of the charge per cubic feet of your items varies depending on the time of year. Storage is more expensive in the latter half of the year due to the demands of the holiday shopping season. If your items sell slowly and are in storage for over 6 months or a year, depending on the item, you will be charged a long-term fee. This does not apply to single items; rather, the long-term storage fee only applies to items in bulk.

Before you get discouraged about the costs of shipping and handling, know that there is a key difference here between individual selling plans and professional selling plans. With an individual selling plan, an extra $0.99 is levied against the cost of your item in exchange for the FBA service.

Professional selling plans allow you as the seller to keep that $0.99, preserving and strengthening your profit margin.

To avoid storage fees, keep the dates of inventory clean-up in mind. Amazon goes through its inventory on August 15th and February 15th; so as you are planning on dates to restock, consider how close you are to running into one of those dates.

Chapter 9 Your First Sales

One of the hardest parts of making decent earnings with online retail is picking the products you will be selling. For many, this can simply be things they find around their homes, at yard sales, garage sales, auctions, thrift stores, and other opportunities that arise. For others, especially those hoping to move in bulk, it is often better to find a reliable wholesale source. We will discuss that later in the book. For now, I want you to consider getting your toes wet first.

Sell Your Used Goods First

Before you go out and buy 1,000 beanie-babies to resell through Amazon's FBA program, let's take the time to get your toes wet and simultaneously declutter your home. Like most of us, I'm sure you have quite a bit of stuff in your house that you no longer need or want. This is a great opportunity to make some extra money while learning how FBA works. So dig out your closets, cupboards, storage spaces, etc., and set aside items that are in decent condition but are no longer any use to you. These are going to become your first shipments to Amazon. It is very easy to get started with just movies, video games, and books. Media items are great because they tend to sell well, the fees related to weight are low, and they are hard to really damage during a shipment.

From there, you'll want to make sure all your items are clean, in working condition, and that you've found a box large enough to ship your entire pile to Amazon. Since you're starting with items you already own, the profit is going to 100% even if it is a low profit. This is a great way to learn the ins and outs without making a huge purchasing mistake first.

To value your items, it is really as simple as making a list of everything you have, and checking each item against what is currently available on Amazon. Consider shipping as part of the overall price (customers will!), and write down the lowest price each item is available for on Amazon from other FBA sellers. (There will be a Fulfillmeny by Amazon logo telling you who the other FBA sellers are).

Using this list of items and prices, you should see that some items are simply not worth selling on Amazon. If you take a video game and look it up on Amazon to find that there are 10 sellers selling it for $0.01 in Like New condition, it's safe to say you can put that back on your shelf or donate it to a thrift store. There are other ways you could exchange them, such as used book/music/game stores, but most owners at these places are not going to give you much in return. However, even a lot of small $2-5 items are worth listing as you're getting your toes wet or if you are able to move a large enough quantity of items with high enough profits to justify the $40 per month that it costs to have a Pro Merchant account. Remember that you can use http://salecalc.com to get a better idea of what your items will ultimately bring you after all costs and fees are paid.

Setting Up Your FBA Account

Now that you have a pile of items and the prices you want to sell them for, it's time to actually get started on your adventure down the Fulfilment by Amazon road. Pick the first of these items you want to list, as you'll need an item to list to sign up as a seller.

If you have an Amazon account already, and you probably do, you can use this as your account for both selling and buying. Don't worry if you have a funny username. You will be prompted to choose a display name during sign up for a seller's account. If you don't have an Amazon account, now is the time to get one. Luckily, the process is simple and doesn't require much in the way of a tutorial.

Once logged into your account, you can click on your "My Account" link, which is typically going to be near the top right of the page. From this page, select "My Other Accounts." You should see a "Seller Account" link within the list; click on this and it will take you to the page with directions to setup a seller account on Amazon.

You will be prompted to sign up as an individual or a professional seller. We briefly discussed the paid, "Pro" program. For now, it probably suffices to use the "free" seller's account.

The next step is to list an item. Yes, you list an item before even finishing the rest of your seller's account signup. This should be fairly simple for you. You'll be asked what category you want to list an item in, and you'll be able to look your item up. If it is already for sale on Amazon, and it probably is, you should be able to select it from a list with thumbnails. Find the one that matches your product as close as possible. From here, you'll be asked to note the condition of the item. From the condition drop down menu, you can choose New, Like New, Very Good, Good, Fair, Poor, etc. Be honest about this. We'll discuss the different types of conditions you can choose shortly.

On the follow page, you'll be asked for a price. You should have this ready on your list. Next is your shipping method. Here you will be able to click, "I want Amazon to ship and provide customer service for my items if they sell." You will also be able to click a box saying that you want Amazon to remember this preference for new listings to come. There's no reason you can't sell and ship some of your items yourself and have Amazon handle others, though. Click the "continue" button, and Amazon will once again ask you to log into your account for security purposes.

The next page is where you will get to setup a display name. These will be displayed next to the listings that belong to your products, and the name should be something professional and approachable. You cannot have a display name that someone else has already used, so you may have to get a bit creative.

Accept the terms of agreement, and then let Amazon walk you through adding in your financial information, such as credit card. If you already have any credit or debit cards associated with your account, you will be able to select these from a menu. If not, you'll have to add a new card. Once this is done, you will be requested to verify your identify over the telephone by inputting your number and clicking "Call now!" You should get a phone call within a minute, and a verification number should appear on the screen. This number will be given over the phone to the automated system, and after a short minute on the phone, you should be allowed to continue with your setup on Amazon as a seller. (NOTE: This financial information is for YOU to make payments to AMAZON in the event that your seller account goes in the negative or you sign up for other services. It is NOT the setup for getting payments. We will cover that later.)

The next step is to review your listing and approve it. Because you've opted for Fulfillment by Amazon, your item will not go up for sale immediately. Instead you'll be asked to agree to Amazon's terms of services once more and then prompted to "Get started with Fulfillment by Amazon." This will bring you through a number of video tutorials that you can watch. I advise that you take the time to watch them at some point, even if you don't do so right away.

At the bottom, you will be able to click a button that says, "Send items to Amazon." You will not immediately have to ship anything to them, but it will ask if you want to ship "stickerless" items or "Stickered" items. "Stickered" inventory consists of used items that will require a sticker barcode generated by Amazon to be sold through the FBA program. You can pay Amazon to sticker your items for you if you wish, but keep in mind that this raises your costs. "Stickerless" items must be new items that have a product barcode on them. "Stickerless" items are "co-mingled" with the same items from other sellers. Because these items are all brand new, Amazon can simply store them together and ship any of them out regardless of the actual seller, which in turn means less storage costs. You may want to take advantage of this down the road, just be sure not to apply it to your used items. That won't work. We will cover stickering in more detail later, so keep this concept in mind.

From here, you'll be asked once again if you want your item to be fulfilled by Amazon. Allow this, and on the following page do not click "convert" or "convert and send." You will do this later, once you've stocked your inventory and prepped your shipment. Your item(s) will simply sit in your inventory as inactive until you're ready.

Your seller account is technically ready to go. The next step is listing the rest of your products.

Listing Products

The one part FBA won't cover for you is listing all of your items. You still have to take the time to build each listing, write a brief description, add images if you choose, and add a price. The process is simple, but it can be time consuming if you're selling a lot of items individually (rather than in large quantities).

First, pull up your list of items (whether it's on paper or in Excel) and start from the top. I suggest having a column in your list that helps you realize what has been listed already and what hasn't, just in case you aren't able to list all items in one sitting. The easiest method to find your product is probably to type the product name in the search bar at Amazon.com, and find the product that best fits the item you're selling. From here, you should see a "Have one to sell?" link at the top-left area of the page.

Alternatively, you can use the inventory section on your seller's dashboard by selecting the link that reads, "Add a Listing" under the "Inventory" menu. The search engine that appears here will allow you to attempt to find what you're selling. If the product has some sort of identification number, this is the ideal method to find what you are selling. This is especially common on books with ISBNs and barcodes. Some items will not have an identification number or any type of barcode, though, and you'll have to simply try your best to find the one that matches your product. Keep in mind that you have a small description box where you can add notes should you place a product in a listing that isn't a 100% perfect match, especially if color is the only difference. Try to always disclose this information.

On the following page, you'll be prompted to input text regarding almost all the information on the product that you could possibly need to include. The form is easy and simple to follow, and it takes no time to setup your listings. The only reason it is time consuming is because you're going to be selling hundreds of items and making killer profits in no time. Let's discuss some of the fields.

SKU:
One of the fields will be for an "SKU." This number is intended to help with keeping your inventory in order. It is highly advised that you create a SKU for everything, especially items that you need to sticker later. Because Amazon creates SKUs randomly if you don't do so manually, letting them handle the SKUs themselves is almost always going to be a headache since the stickers don't always print in the correct order of how you've organized them. I would use a five-digit code and start your first product off as 00001 and move forward from there. Keep a note about which number you last used, as SKUs cannot be repeated, and the next time you list items, you'll want to start where you left off to help keep everything proficiently organized.

Condition:
The next item is a drop down menu that lets you pick the condition of your item. There are several types of conditions to choose from.

NEW – An item that has never been used whatsoever. For items that come sealed, this means the item is still sealed. For items that don't come sealed, this means absolutely perfect condition. If it comes in a box, the box should be included.

USED – LIKE NEW – In near-perfect condition. Should be as a new looking as an item that's never been used.

USED – VERY GOOD – Clean items with only very minimal wear.

USED – GOOD – For items that have scuffing or small imperfections, the "Good" condition is ample. Any imperfections should be purely cosmetic. An item must function 100% to be considered in "GOOD" condition.

USED – ACCEPTABLE – Clearly not in the best of condition but still fully functional, such as a used text book with highlighter in it.

With all of these conditions, you'll be able to leave a note regarding condition and any other details you may wish to portray. Try to be thorough and honest when choosing conditions and leaving notes. A simple note saying, "Highlighted text, but fully readable," is suitable.

It's important to understand that people are willing to buy things in less-than-perfect condition if they still work well, so lying about this isn't really helpful anyway. On the other hand, if an item is poorly categorized within these conditions or the notes suggest something that isn't true, you are more likely to see items being returned or your seller account getting poor feedback from buyers.

You will see that some sellers simply use the same bit of text on the condition note over and over. While this is a great way to cut back on time-consuming tasks, it is often misleading and not helpful to the potential customer. Take the time to write these in. It only takes a few seconds to determine the quality of your product.

Price:

The next part should be easy, but that isn't always the case. You should have already put together a list of prices when sorting and valuing your items. Remember, the number you should write down is the lowest available price from another Fulfilled by Amazon seller. In this section, Amazon will provide you with the lowest price for your item. There is the option to "MATCH" these low prices. Never. Ever. Use. This.

The problem with using price matching to price items is that the cheapest one available for your item could be a destroyed mess where yours is practically new. Additionally, you must remember that those selling FBA are your direct competition, not every seller on Amazon. So it really pays to go to the product listings and see what the competition actually looks like. There's no reason you need to sell your Like New item for less than an item covered in dirt and grime, or something far worse.

Instead, you should be pricing your items based on their condition and what you believe people will pay for it. The lowest price isn't always the item that sells, and sometimes we cannot sell items as cheap as other providers without losing money. In the end, you can always adjust your price later if it seems like an item might sell better at a different price point. On the same note, pushing for the lowest price is likely only going to force other sellers to lower their prices, driving down the perceived value of your item even further.

If you have a rare or expensive item, don't be tempted to way undercut the only other listing. If there's a listing for a rare item priced at $200, listing yours at $100 only works to drive down the market value. Instead, you should price competitively without undercutting the value of the item; anything else is just counter-productive. Some rare items may be worth a lot but only have a limited number of interested buyers. In these scenarios, you may just have to wait for the item to finally sell or consider another selling method.

Again, keep in mind that your competition isn't as broad as a seller that isn't using Fulfillment by Amazon. Because you're allowing them to ship your items, shoppers with Prime membership perks and those looking to score free shipping on orders over $49 are more likely to buy your items even if they aren't quite as cheap as the lowest available in the same condition. Use this to your advantage when pricing, because your most direct competition is only other listings that are using FBA.

When it's possible, being the only seller that is working through Fulfillment by Amazon is going to be a great advantage. Some people will even take the time to locate popular items without any sellers using FBA, and because they can offer the perks that others aren't offering, that item can usually sell quicker and for a little more money.

Keep in mind that it doesn't matter too much if the product is cheaper on another website. Your competition is within Amazon, not with the entire world wide web. So even if you find the same product for half the cost, if the lowest on Amazon is higher, you can still price within that range. You might even considered buying the item from another site if it's cheap enough for you to make a profit.

Setting the price can be the easiest or the hardest part of working for yourself through FBA, and it's important not to be lazy and simply list at the lowest possible at all times.

Quantity:
The next item on your product listing form is the quantity of the item you are selling. Even if you have multiples of the same items and the condition is not the same, Amazon will require you to list them together. This is unfortunate because it makes it difficult to be totally transparent and almost forces you to list a like new item as something less than like new.

Restock Date:
Unless you intend to restock the same items over and over, leave this field blank. This is only useful if you restock on a regular basis.

Other Fields
There are other fields sometimes related to the category. For example, a book listing will allow you to add in information concerning the country of publication. These should all be self-explanatory or easily searched when you're unsure. Often, you will/can simply ignore these optional questions either way.

Shipping Method:
Lastly, you will enter the shipping method you wish to use. There will be an option for having Amazon fulfill the order. This is what you will likely check.

Images:
Likely we've already passed this section, but one thing worth noting is that if there are no stock images available (and even if there are), it may be a good idea to add images to your listing or even submit them to the main listing so the item doesn't have a "no image shown" icon. This is important because images help buyers make a connection with a product before they purchase it. Most people don't want to

purchase an item they can't see. If you have the patience and time, or if you only stock a handful of items, you may want to invest in the effort of taking photographs for all of your listings. These can greatly help to increase sales.

Save and Finish

Once everything is entered, you will click on "Save and Finish" to complete your listing. You will be given the option to "Send Inventory" or "Go Back." You will want to click "Send Inventory."

Add to Shipment

Following submitting your first product, you will be asked to confirm your address and add your item to a shipment. Since you don't have a shipment setup yet, your option will be to "Create a New Shipment." Click this and start a shipment. As you continue to list products, you will have the option to join them into an existing shipment in many cases. In some cases, you may not be able to do this and will be required to open a new shipment.

Take a moment to understand this faucet of FBA. Not all items can be sent to the same fulfillment center at once. As such, as you create shipments, you may be forced to ship several different bundles of items to multiple locations.

In your inventory, you may notice that there is a four-digit code next to your items. This code represents the fulfillment center appropriate for the item. Since not all items go to the same fulfillment centers, you may be working on shipping several boxes at once. Try to make sure you're keeping this stuff organized correctly. Do not completely pack your items yet, as we'll need to add the SKU stickers first. It is wise, however, to place them in a box to get an idea of the total weight of your package. Write down this weight when you're finished.

After listing your last item and choosing to add it to a shipment or create a new shipment, you will have the option to "Save and Continue" on this same page. Do this only once you've listed all your items! If you need to list another item, click the "Home" link and repeat the process above. Otherwise, you may be wasting money shipping small packages when you could send out only a few large ones and help keep down your operation costs, or have to deal with the headache of canceling and adjusting.

Chapter 10 How and Why to Private Label!

There are several different ways to sell products on Amazon. One of the most popular ways is through retail arbitrage where sellers visit retail stores (they spend HOURS in there or visit their online stores) and find items that are heavily discounted to buy them in BULK (or at only a few units at a time) and then go on to sell them for a profit on Amazon after packaging and sending in the products themselves. Retail arbitrage is a great way to get started in the business of selling on Amazon as you learn the ropes and get hands on experience with it but unless you simply don't have the capital for private label we would say just start with private labelling as you will eventually get to it if you're any part successful at retail arbitrage. Another common way of selling on Amazon is through buying products from wholesalers. This process called wholesaling is where sellers buy established products cheaply through established wholesalers and then send and list these products on Amazon. Another way people get into selling on Amazon which isn't as common is when they are already selling products through their own stores or business and decide to make them available on Amazon.

One of the most lucrative strategies for selling on Amazon is private labeling. Private labelling is generally considered the apex of selling when it comes to Amazon as it is the most complex (and by complex that simply means it has more steps to it than the other methods do). With retail arbitrage and wholesaling, the products you sale are generally not sustainable over the long term. The issue with retail arbitrage is that you need to keep finding products that are heavily discounted and in stock, this takes up a lot of your time and doesn't result in a true passive income stream. A lot of people are doing retail arbitrage as well so then retail arbitrager's start getting into price listing wars with each other on Amazon. This kills what little profit margins they had to begin with and there are other issues such as getting product listings hijacked etc., which is a whole other topic on their own. With wholesalers, anyone can find the same wholesaler and decide to purchase the products from them and start reselling on Amazon. This results in a loss of sales and will most likely turn into a price war as well, with profit margins decreasing once more. It isn't quite true that private labelling is the apex of selling on Amazon because once you are brand and sales are really established, you have the opportunity to then start wholesaling your product (so people will be coming to you to buy your product in bulk to sell) and also look for opportunities to get your product into retail stores making the circle whole. This comes up a lot later down the track so it's nothing that you need to concern yourself with.

With private labelling however, you pay a manufacturer (or a reseller of a manufacturer if you're not careful!) to produce items straight from their factory line and they slap your own private label to the products. From there you *can* have the factory package and label the products and deliver the products directly to Amazon's warehouses or if you would prefer, you can choose to send your products to companies based in the US who will then do the packaging and labelling for you before shipping it off to Amazon. From here you put up a product listing on Amazon which will include the product description, photos, and other similar details such as dimensions, weight and so forth. When your shipment lands in Amazon's warehouse, begin marketing and execute the launch phase for the product. Sit back, relax, and monitor sales.

Private label selling is nothing new in terms of business and it's likely you've bought private label products frequently in the past. Many generic items in supermarkets may be produced from the exact same source: the value brand milk you buy at Walmart and Costco may have come from the same cow at one point in time. Some supermarkets may even sell the same product within their own store. It's just that the exterior in terms of the branding, labeling, and packaging are different. More blatant attempts of this are evidenced in independent discount stores that might, for example, sell the exact same bottle of superglue only with different packaging or labels. These identical products may even be involved in pricings wars between the respective brands that sell them.

Amazon has actually taken hold of the private label game as it sells an entire range of items with its own logo and label. Fortunately though, this kind of private label selling is open to you as well. Whereas before you might have only sold such products to independent stores, you can now sell directly to a large mass of consumers by using Amazon as a platform. FBA provides a unique opportunity because it gives you the tools to research different markets, identify what is popular, and what is not so popular, and it gives you a place to list an item where customers are already looking for similar products and are willing to spend their cash. What you first need to do is pick the correct product, fill a need in the product's market and supply it to the horde of consumers. So enough with the frivolities, let's get down to the real meat and guts of this business and what you purchased this book for!

Chapter 11 Amazon FBA Seller Pricing and Repricing Tools

Determining how much to sell a product becomes easy with the use of pricing and repricing tools. These are used by sellers to list, scout and reprice products.

To begin with, let's consider Amazon's native app.

Amazon Seller App
Amazon has now created its own seller app to help Amazon sellers. The Amazon Seller mobile app can make your life easier as an Amazon seller to instantly update your FBA inventory, find and list new products online and answer customer inquiries.

The following are the Amazon Seller app features that make this app useful:

Update Inventory - Easily manage your Amazon FBA inventory: You can find, sort and filter product items, update your selling prices and change item quantities quickly from your mobile phone.

Source New Items to Sell - By entering product names or scanning barcodes, you can now compare existing selling prices, product sales rank and the customer reviews of the specific products on Amazon.

Calculate The Potential Earning of Products Before Selling - Add product price information to find out the expected potential earning of products.

List New Products to Sell - Make new product listings on Amazon instantly and conveniently.

Respond to Customers Inquiries - Give impressive customer support by replying quickly to customers inquiries.

View your current earnings - See how much earnings you currently have and when you'll get paid by Amazon.

Get Assistance from Amazon - Use the app to get in touch with seller assistance using email or chat.

Download the Amazon Seller App: If you want to try the Amazon Seller app, you can download it for free. You can get it from Google Play for Android, Apple for iOS and also from the Amazon App Store if you are using an Amazon device.

Choosing which seller app to work with is solely based on personal taste and preference. In some cases, there are some important features that you can get from non-Amazon apps. However, it will require you to spend more. If you are just okay with that, you can find out below which app can work best for you and your budget.

1. Listing Tools

   Listing of products through the Amazon Seller Central can be time-consuming especially if you'll be listing more than 50 items a month. Listing tools are used to automate and speed up the process of putting up your inventory on Amazon.

ASellertool - This allows you to batch large quantity of items all at once and it supports FBA shipment management and label printing. You can register the Amazon Batch Listing software after registering your Amazon MWS (Marketplace Web Service) account to Asellertool service.

Listtee - This tool offers a simple listing software that links to all US and UK Amazon FBA warehouses. With this tool, you can replenish items and print single labels. It also has a feature on SKU detection to avoid listing of the same item twice, thus reduce listing errors.

Neatoscan - This tool is used to sell on multiple platforms. If later on, you decide to sell aside from your Amazon Seller account, then you may try the Inventory Manager tool. This tool integrates your online business so you can save time and costs while increasing productivity. The features include prescanning and receiving, inventory management, shipping, reports and FBA integration.

2. Scouting Tools

Getting a good product should be your main goal whenever you want to list an item on Amazon. To help you make wise decisions about potential inventory, you can use scouting tools. Most of the listing tools are integrated with its scouting tool so that after scouting, the listing could be easy and quick to accomplish.

Asellertool FBA scan - This App is for Android or iPhone gadgets, which can help you in checking the Amazon pricing information by scanning or entering the item's barcode. One good advantage of this App is that it has two scouting modes, the Local Database, and Live Search. The former requires no internet connection or can be used in areas with poor signal wherein the price information is stored in your phone, while the latter is used with internet connection and get real-time Amazon price information including those not found in local databases.

Listtee Scout Rabbit - This App can be availed from Listtee Pro and Enterprise Lite plans. It is another App to bring you the basic FBA pricing data as well as sales rank across all Amazon categories. When scouting for items, product barcodes can be read by Bluetooth scanner, a phone camera and by typing the name of the product.

Neato-scan – Neato-scan has another tool, the Neato-pricer. This tool utilizes a barcode scanner and PDA or iPhone/Android device without a need for internet connection. This helps you to have a quick and easy way to determine the value of the merchandise. It requires you to download first the PDA before you scan all categories.

- **Seller-Engine Profit-bandit App** - This App is considered as the #1 mobile Amazon seller software, which is downloaded either for iPhone or Android phones. Profit Bandit is a tool that helps seller maximize profit, keep an eye on the competition, and save time while making money. Using this App will help you find how much profit you can make from the item you want to sell. It scans the barcode and computes the cost including the FBA fees and you'll get the possible profit.

Scan power Scout - This App provides a real-time data from Amazon and access to the entire catalog. A very useful App because of the information it provides that include data of other FBA sellers such as the number they are selling and the net price after taking out Amazon fees.

- **Scout-pal** - There are two tools that can be used from Scout-pal: the Instant Lookups with a PDA and Live Lookups with a phone. The tools are simple and easy to use whenever you scout for items. You only need to enter the ISBNs or UPCs of an item and the tool will get the information you need. If you have a scanner attached to your device, you can scan it instead of entering the data. Then, you'll see information on the lowest prices in used/new/collectible lists, Amazon price, and sales rank. More so, the Live results will show the market prices and quantities, editions and availability. To easily comprehend the report, you can customize the content and format the details according to your preference.

3. Repricing Tools

With a dynamic marketplace such as the Amazon, updating and keeping your inventory with the right price is necessary. Repricing tools help you automate the process by selecting your criteria and reprice a large number of items within a short amount of time. Most of the repricing tools are offered with a listing tool such as the Neato-Scan Inventory Manager; it is advisable that you evaluate every part of the features and go for the best App for you.

Reprice-It - This tool is a cloud-based system, thus, no software needs to be downloaded. You can access your account anywhere with internet connection. This tool allows you to schedule repricing more frequently during peak buying times on Amazon while experimenting with different repricing strategies. Most importantly, this tool has full FBA support and you'll get detailed repricing reports onto your email.

Scan-Power -This App is used by sellers when listing items to sell. It has different features like Evaluate and Reprice for great use of sellers. These features help you calculate the prices based on FBA net price, which includes the price and shipping.

Sellery - This tool from Seller-Engine is used to help sellers compete and maximize profits. It features the Sellery's on-demand, per item pricing preview where you can create new pricing rules, pick any item in your inventory and preview your pricing strategies. With this App, you can prevent price mistakes because floor price calculation is automated and item-specific. It includes Amazon fees, FBA and shipping costs aside from the margin you want so you can come up with an accurate minimum price.

Amazon FBA Tools are definitely a must-have on your phone when you start selling on Amazon. An extra fee for the Apps will ensure that you are pricing your items properly and competitively on Amazon. No need to guess any price for your item. If you want to get the highest possible margin for your inventory, make sure that your pricing is calculated based on accurate data and information.

Materials Needed For Your Shipment

Starting out selling on Amazon will require a few materials that are needed in order to send your products to an Amazon warehouse. Some tools are very necessary while others will just make your life as a seller easier. Investing in tools that will increase productivity is a great idea and should be considered.

1 - Boxes
Let's begin with materials that are necessary. We're going to need shipping boxes. For your first shipment I recommend you collect free boxes from anywhere you can get them such as local stores, Craigslist and friends are all good options. Once you begin sending more and more shipments are required then buying boxes would be a better idea. All home improvement stores sell boxes that are perfect for FBA. Try and stick with small or medium boxes and only use large boxes if your shipment will be bulky.

2 - Packing Tape

Packing Tape and a Tape Gun are going to very important tools to pack your boxes together. You can buy these anywhere and at a cheap price. If you start shipping out more boxes then consider buying tape in bulk instead of single rolls. The minimum tape size that you should use is 2.2 mil. However, those tapes that are bigger and larger will stick better on the box.

3 - Measuring Tape

You need to measure the boxes you are about to send out to Amazon. Every box needs to be measured before you print a shipping label. You can get an inexpensive measuring tape at your local thrift store. Many retail stores have some affordable ones.

4 - Printer

The Dymo Label Printer is perfect for FBA labels and you will save money since you won't be buying ink anymore. However, for starters, you can use a toner laser printer since their prints don't smudge.

For the complete printing and labeling information, please see Amazon's printing guidelines.

5 - Labels

For printing your product label barcodes, you will need a standard 30-up address label. I highly recommend the Avery 18160 and 5160 address labels. However, you could also find other generic address labels that will work as good as the branded one.

If you don't want to spend more money, printing your barcodes on a white blank sheet of paper and using a tape to stick them on the boxes, can work as well. However, the time and effort for you to do it yourself are not so worth it. Address labels are just cheap, just buy them and save yourself from trouble.

Just make sure your labels are printed and placed properly on your boxes or products.

To learn more about proper labeling, please view this YouTube tutorial by Amazon: How to Label Products for Fulfillment by Amazon.

6 - Scales
Shipping scales are going to be needed to accurately calculate the weight for your boxes. At first using a bathroom or a kitchen scale will work fine but I highly recommend a shipping scale to properly weigh your products.

7 - Poly Bags
Consider as well having the poly bags since you will need to put many of your products enclosed with poly bags.

With these items, you will have what is needed for shipping. It may be a little costly at first but these are only initial investments that will surely pay off in the long run. Always remember to follow all of Amazon's rules and regulations.

How To Ship Inventory to Amazon Fulfillment Centers

In this section, I will discuss more how to ship products to Amazon, since they are the ones who will handle individual shipping to buyers. All we have to do is send our products to the Amazon warehouse.

Before we ship anything to Amazon we need to make sure our products are packaged and labeled. We cannot just send them products with no encasing so make sure your product packing is secure. Once the items are ready then we are going to have to pack them into boxes to be shipped to Amazon. Make sure to print shipping labels for your boxes that can be found in the Inventory section that will include a list of products within the box and the quantity.

It is very advisable to use as few boxes as possible to avoid any possible loss. Furthermore, make sure to protect your products when packing with foam, air pillows or sheets of paper. Finally, check the boxes to see if they are sealed and your products will not move during shipping. When it comes to choosing a carrier you are free to choose any carrier with any shipping speed you wish. Just make sure to provide the tracking numbers when using your own carrier.

As mentioned before, make sure to print shipping labels for all your boxes. Go to the Shipping Queue to print them out and attach the labels to the outside of the box. The labels will show the destination address and return address. In some cases, the tracking number can also be shown, if you are using an Amazon carrier. This will make sure that all your products are packaged for protection against any damage during shipping or storage and that all units follow Amazon's labeling and requirements.

When a product is shipped out to a customer your name does not appear on any item labels nor shipping labels but on the packing slip that will be found inside the box. This is the only reference the buyer has that the product came from you.

Amazon also accepts shipments from other countries to their warehouses. However, the seller will have to arrange the imports of his product, go through customs and lastly get the products delivered to an Amazon warehouse. Amazon will not serve as an importer for your imported products, they will not take responsibility for any taxes or fees related to your import nor will they provide a tax number for you. The seller is responsible for dealing with all government agencies that relate to his import and has to provide prepaid delivery to the Amazon warehouse. Also, Amazon does not provide any quality check to your products unless they are obviously and visibly damaged. If the item is labeled as "used" then it is understandable that it may have minor damages and will not be checked.

Dealing with customs, shipping charges, and all the different taxes is a total problem. Fortunately, there are many companies, referred to as freight forwarders, which could handle everything on your behalf. You simply connect your forwarder with your manufacturer and they can get all the details taken care of.

You can check the following freight forwarders and their services and see which one can best satisfy your requirements:

- Forest-Shipping - *Frequently Asked Questions for FBA shipment*
- Riversource-Logistics - *How It Works, Support Center*
- Adstral-Fulfilment - *Amazon Fulfillment*
- Shapiro - *Amazon FBA*
- *FBA-forward* - Services
- **AMZ**-transit - **Services**

Once again, Amazon does its best to make selling as easy as possible. All you have to do is get your products to the warehouse in good condition while following the requirements set by Amazon and we will be good to go.

How Amazon Handle Returns and Warranty?

Returns are common in this business. Maybe the buyer expected your product to be different, possibly damaged due to everyday reasons or they decided they just don't want your product anymore. Don't let it affect the way you feel about your product nor the way you conduct business. As long as you are keeping returns at a minimum then you're doing just fine.

With that said, we must know how to handle returns and the procedures that come with them. Amazon has always made it easy for its customers when it comes to return, they will process the whole return. Once the product reaches Amazon they will determine if the product is eligible for return or not. They will however usually accept units if they are returned within a certain time frame.

When the customer is issued the returned then Amazon will charge your seller account for the product including any taxes in order to reimburse the returnee. Now if the product is damaged and is found unsellable then Amazon will reimburse you, this also applies if the item was lost or never arrived at the buyer.

The Customer Return Timeline for most products is 30 days and 90 days for Baby products. For products that are returned within the timeline, they will firstly have the product checked for any damage that would make the product unsellable. Products that are still in sellable condition will be placed back into your inventory in the warehouse. While any products that appear to be damaged will not be placed back into your inventory and you will be fully reimbursed for the item. There are certain cases where

Amazon will not take responsibility and you will not be reimbursed for the item.

Amazon will always consider all cases that are returned outside the return timeline and from time to time accept returns. If Amazon decides to accept the return then the same procedure would be followed as if the item was returned within the timeline, you will be fully reimbursed as well.

Let's go over what makes an item sellable or unsellable. An item that is still sellable will be added back to your inventory while any items that are considered unsellable will be placed in your "Unfulfillable Inventory" if Amazon in certain cases does not reimburse you. An item is unsellable if it is not in the same condition that it was originally shipped as or if the product is opened, damaged, defective or special cases when Amazon finds your product unsuitable.

Amazon once again shows how they take care of everyone working with them. Returning is made easy for the buyer and the seller. Just remember that returns are part of being a seller so get through them smoothly and continue selling.

Chapter 12 Driving Traffic to Your Product

By now you should have your product listing page built and your products on the way to the fulfillment center or waiting there ready to be sold! In this section I will be covering the most effective ways that you can start driving traffic to your product to make your initial sales. It's time to start making money!

Website & Blog

Although your product is selling on Amazon, there are a bunch of reasons to build a separate website for your brand and product:

- Helps build your brand

- Makes your company look very professional

- Allows you to further communicate with your customer base

- *Allows you to collect email addresses from customers*

Within your website you can build a blog which has numerous benefits, such as ranking in Google for your topics and placing you as an authority in your niche.

There are a variety of companies that you can use to start a website, but here are the key things that you will need to start:

- Website domain for your brand

- HOSTING

- Word Press

- *Basic or premium theme*

This should all cost less than $100, which is a small price to pay for the benefit that it can have for your brand and product. Ultimately, this will help drive traffic to your Amazon product and increase brand awareness.

Amazon Ads

The best way to start immediately driving traffic to your product is by using Amazon Sponsored Ads. This is the easiest and quickest way to start generating revenue for your new business. These ads are shown throughout the Amazon search pages, and you will be charged for these ads on a cost-per-click basis. You do not create the ads yourself because the ad information taken directly from your product page.

Auto vs. Manual Campaign

There are two types of campaigns that can be set up, but it's important that you only run one at a time.

Auto campaign:

With an auto campaign you don't have control over the keywords being targeted or the cost per click for each keyword. I recommend using this type of campaign in the initial stages because it will give you keywords that you might not have thought of and may make sales from. You can then target these keywords within a manual campaign.

Manual campaign:

After running an auto campaign I strongly recommend running a manual campaign which will allow you to target specific keywords and have more control over your cost-per-click and overall ad spend. You can use the keywords that you discovered in your initial keyword research and ones discovered when running the auto campaign.

Setting Up Your Amazon ads

- Login to your Amazon Seller Central account.
- Go the 'Advertising' tab in the menu bar.
- Click on 'Campaign Manager'.
- Click on 'Create Campaign'.
- Enter your campaign name, I recommend using the product name.
- Set your daily budget - something you are initial comfortable with, I recommend starting at around $15 per day to begin with.
- Add a start date.
- Select your targeting type - Auto or Manual campaign.
- Click 'Continue to the Next Step'
- Create an Ad Group
- Select the product you want to advertise.
- *Select a default bid based on the average winning bid.*

Once set up, your ads can be live within 30 minutes - you can start making sales that very day!

Optimizing Amazon ads: If you see a keyword getting a lot of clicks but little sales, it is probably best to either reduce the bid on this keyword or even remove the keyword if it is performing very poorly.

Ideally, you should be able to run ads that are profitable, and this is the result of selling products at a slightly higher price point. Remember to keep optimizing and improving in order to improve your cost of ads per sale. Keep running your ads even if you are only breaking even - the more sales you make, the higher Amazon will rank your product in the search results. This will allow you to make organic sales without ad spend in the future.

Other Methods of Driving Traffic

- Search engine advertising on Google and Bing
- Press releases
- Facebook ads
- Pinterest ads
- Coupon and deal sites

Chapter 13 How to Get Ungated in Restricted Category?

A lot of bundles that are sold on Amazon through FBA include health products, groceries and beauty products. These products are restricted to be sold by approved sellers. You can still make your own bundles by combining products listed in ungated categories- baby products, housewares, garden and lawn products, kitchenware, and many more.

However, if you are not an approved supplier for health and beauty, groceries, etc.; you can still utilize the great opportunity to apply for the same. You can get approved in these categories easily.

You can sell millions of products from your Amazon Seller Account. But, some products fall in the restricted category. This is done by Amazon to control the sale of inferior quality products by sellers through their website. You can overcome most of these restrictions if you have good quality products to sell, while many other restrictions are not easy to overcome.

Restricted Categories
The gated or restricted categories can be overcome by taking permission from Amazon to sell your goods in these categories. Most sellers would just keep away from these gated categories assuming that they need to be a huge company to sell in these categories. But in actuality, the process of application is really uncomplicated. You would not face any problem if you follow the rules listed by Amazon. If you are able to prove that you are sourcing your goods from an authentic source, and follow the guidelines of Amazon,

you would not face any problem in gaining access to these categories.

Build reputation

The first requirement is that you must be a pro seller. You need to pay a subscription fee monthly to access the Amazon marketplace. The individual sellers of US and basic sellers of UK cannot apply for this. Also, you must have a sales history to build credibility. You can also show your sales history with positive reviews on Amazon FBA.

Have a ready stock of inventory

You must have some inventory ready to sell in the restricted category. Amazon would not wait for you to procure your stock if you are in the process of "thinking" to make sales in the gated categories. They must know that you are a legitimate supplier with geared up inventory. It does not mean that you have to buy huge quantities, but at least a decent amount of stock to show if required. You can even talk to your supplier to negotiate refund policies if you have doubts. If Amazon does not grant permission for the gated categories, you must have some options to sell your goods somewhere else, like on eBay.

Understand other categories individually

All categories have different requirements for approval. Also, Amazon keeps changing the requirements for granting permission to different categories. When the process of application begins, you will get only two days amid each step to submit the information requested by Amazon. You must ensure that you have all your documents in place to avoid delay in submission or cancellation of your application. If you have any doubts, you must contact Seller support beforehand.

Providing images

Some categories require you to submit at least five images of the products to Amazon to gain approval. You can submit images of any of the products but they should comply with the guidelines of Amazon. You do not need to hire a professional photographer to click good photos. You can use any good software to comply with the image guidelines.

Providing invoices

Some categories of products require you to submit the invoices to show that you have bought your goods from a reliable source. Amazon usually requires you to submit three invoices procured from various stores. The invoices should show the name of your business and address, the name, phone number and address of the supplier, quantity bought.

Flat file upload

Some categories require you to submit a flat file of your goods. Flat file implies an Excel Spreadsheet that can be uploaded to the Seller Central so that you can list your products in one go rather than listing them individually. You can procure the templates from Amazon. At least five products are required for this and some of them have to be parent-child goods.

Gaining access to gated categories is not complicated. It is just elaborate. If you comply by the requirements, your process of application will go smoothly.

Other restrictions of Amazon

There are some categories of restricted products which cannot be accessed. It is difficult to get permission for these categories. If you try to make your own listings, you may end up violating Amazon's policies and your account may be blocked. Thus, you must be aware of these strictly restricted categories.

Restricted Brands

Some brands are completely restricted to be sold by other sellers to avoid duplicity or fake products. Some of the examples of such brands include Apple, Burberry and MAC cosmetics. You can list used items of these brands, but not as a new item. Before proceeding for listing restricted products you have doubts about, you must clarify your doubts first. You can even try to contact the brands directly to clarify your doubts.

FBA Restrictions

When you are selling through FBA program of Amazon, you must know about some products which are not allowed to be stored in their warehouse, though you can sell them as an Amazon Merchant. This means that you have to ship them directly from your place.

Some of these products include firearms, razor blades, knives, fireworks, loose gemstones, medicines, etc. In short, anything which is potentially harmful to the warehouse staff cannot be stored at Amazon. But, these restrictions also vary from region to region.

Prohibited Products

Some categories of products are simply not allowed to be sold through Amazon. Some examples are animal products like feathers, fur, ivory, used clothing, e-cigarettes, tobacco products, and of course, live animals.

In brief

You might find many products that are restricted on Amazon. But, in reality, millions products are sold on Amazon. Do not get disheartened if you find the restrictions too elaborate. They are there for your own benefit and of the society at large. You must do the research and ensure that you comprehend the restrictions. If you are not sure about the restrictions on your goods, you can attempt to add it to your account of supplies.

If any listing is associated with your products, Amazon might raise some issues. It is indeed inconvenient. But, you need to take the pain for a few minutes. It will save you the hassle of negotiating refunds from your suppliers.

If there are no listings associated with your products, you can contact the Seller Support to locate any issues linked with your goods.

Chapter 14 Scaling your Amazon FBA Business

In this part, we will discuss how to make an email list for your blog. On the off chance that you converse with any effective blogger, they will reveal to you the significance of having an email list. Having somebody's email will enable you to get in touch with them decisively. It is more probable for individuals to see and tap on your email than it is for them to get some answers concerning your most recent post online which implies you can't neglect the intensity of email and email promoting.

I will show you today how to gather messages through free traffic and pop-ups. Gathering email can be a tedious and an arduous procedure, yet vital.

I will do my best to make it basic for you. Keep in mind that building a decent email rundown will require some serious energy. Additionally, on the grounds that you have figured out how to gather 10,000 messages doesn't mean every one of them will tap on your email.

You have to ensure you are keeping your messages endorsers connected with and hanging tight for the following email, which we will show you in this section. Ultimately, we will additionally manage you on the most proficient method to make probably the most astonishing messages. It will assist you with getting a higher snap through rate. Despite the fact that email showcasing is great, just 30% of individuals will peruse and click your email. We need to ensure we leave no stones unturned to do that and we need an elegantly composed email.

Collecting email

Toward the start of your blogging venture, you won't have a lot of cash to spend on promoting. In this section we will keep everything free assets, which means, you won't need to pay a dime on gathering any messages. Presently there are two fundamental ways for you to acquire messages. The first is through a spring up.

You can utilize email assets like MailChimp to make a free spring up. What spring up will assist you with is the point at which somebody visits your site, they will get a major box directly before them. It will approach them to agree to accept our email list so they could get a free book or something along that line, as we discussed in the past section. Contingent upon your specialty give your readers something of significant worth.

In case you're in the wellness Niche, you can offer your readers free eBooks on the most proficient method to put on muscle. Make sense of the considerable number of requirements and issues individuals have in your specialty. Make a free eBook or a cheat sheet and offer them for nothing. It is an absolute necessity have on your site. Odds are if individuals are on your site as of now, they won't falter to put their email in pop-ups with the expectation of complimentary data.

Your Landing Page

Presently the second method to gather messages is use something many refer to as a greeting page. When you join with mailchimp.com. which is allowed to utilize, you would then be able to begin making free points of arrival for your site. What presentation page will do is help you gather messages through YouTube and different destinations. In the past section, we discussed gathering messages through YouTube. This is the place points of arrival come in.

Make your presentation page through mailchimp.com. At that point duplicate that connection and post it on your YouTube recordings and different sites on the web. Your presentation page will offer a blessing in return for their email. So in the event that you go on to wellness structures and specialty sites you can gradually include your point of arrival there to explicit individuals who are into your specialty. It is additionally an amazing route for you to gather messages on your YouTube recordings and other specialty related sites. You need your point of arrival there ready for action. On the off chance that not, at that point you are passing up a ton of free leads.

Making email
At long last, the fun part, how to make an email and how regularly you ought to send messages to your readers. So the main thing you have to ensure is that you have your appreciated email computerized. In case you're utilizing the administrations, we prescribe mailchimp.com. You ought to have no issue robotizing email since it is exceptionally direct.

At whatever point somebody agrees to accept your email list, the main thing you have to do is ensure you are sending them the blessing you have guaranteed. Your "appreciated" email will be the main robotized email, ensure your "appreciated" email is sent following they enter their email. This would be your robotized email, since you have made you're free to email and computerized it, we will currently discuss the recurrence and the sorts of email you ought to send your supporters.

As to rate, you ought to never email your readers multiple times each week. There are two explanations behind it. To begin with, you will have a lower possibility of winding up in their spam email. Second, your readers won't get irritated by your messages. Subsequently, they won't withdraw.

With respect to messages, update them about the most recent blog and the partner items you need to offer them two times per week. This is a decent principle guideline I like to live by. Not exclusively will they be locked in on the information you give them, yet they will probably turn into your clients. It won't resemble you're shelled with deals pitch constantly. Subsequent to attempting this for quite a long time and years, I can reveal to you this is the best technique for messaging your readers.

On the off chance that you need to have an effective blog, you need your readers drew in through email. You can lose online networking following, yet the messages will live on until the end of time. Some should seriously think about email medieval, however most organizations are running exclusively on email showcasing. Try not to belittle the intensity of email promoting, particularly for bloggers. Utilize these techniques we just discussed in this section to gather messages. Try not to leave any stones unturned on the off chance that you need to make progress in blogging.

Guest Blogging

As of recently in this book, we have talked about a great deal of approaches to get traffic to your blog. The present part, we're going to discuss the granddaddy of all, visitor blogging. Posting your article on another person's blog, otherwise called visitor blogging is a standout amongst the most ideal ways for you to create traffic to your blog.

Presently there are several things to recall before you begin posting your online journals on other individuals' sites. The main thing you need to ensure is that you have a few online journals all alone website before you post on others. Let's be honest, nobody needs new bloggers to post on their site, get a few certifications and compose an incredible blog or two develop a resume. When you've figured out how to post two or three online journals all alone website, at that point you can begin reviewing visitor writes so as to create more traffic and to get some reputation in your specialty.

The sooner you begin visitor blogging, the better it will be for your image. It will enable you to make more backlinks, however it will likewise enable you to draw in more readers to your blog. Another extraordinary thing about this strategy is that if the site you posted on gets new readers, the odds of the new readers to visit and turn into a reader of your blog would be exceptionally high. Presently you should simply discover individuals who will enable you to post on their site, that is the thing that we will show you in this section.

Be precise with your niche

Before we move further into this section, we have to clear up two or three things. On the off chance that you need to take advantage of your visitor blogging attempts, at that point you have to ensure that the site which you have chosen to visitor present on is connected on your specialty. It can't be "kind of" related with your specialty, it must be unequivocally identified with your specialty.

For example, in the event that your specialty is tied in with weight training, at that point you discover a yoga site searching for a visitor blogger, don't proceed to attempt and post on their website as you won't increase any traffic from it. Kindly remember this progression as it is basic for your achievement in the blogging scene. You won't win any new readers from it. On the off chance that the "kind of" related site chooses to post your article on their site, they may lose a few readers and you may likewise lose a ton of regard in the blogging scene.

Discovering sites to post on

Before you feel free to discover locales to post on, ensure that the site you find is progressing nicely. The most ideal approach to see whether the sites are getting a ton of connected readers is to perceive what number of social offers a particular article or the site is getting.

That is a standout amongst the most ideal approaches to see whether the site is a go-go or no-go. Beyond any doubt you can post it on every one of the spots conceivable yet this will just make you look frantic for traffic That isn't what you need to look like in case you will have a long haul continued business. Presently there are a great deal of approaches to discover sites to post on, however the best site is clearly Google.

Simply look "Present a visitor post." If you see a site in your specialty which is tolerating visitor posts, email them. It is as basic as it sounds. They may request that you send a connection to your ongoing post so ensure you are composing the most ideal articles.

Composing the post

When you at long last found your site to post your blog on and they have acknowledged you, it will be a great opportunity to compose the article. Contingent upon the webpage and their readers, your composing must be at a similar dimension as the site you will be visitor blogging on. This will enable you to pull in more readers to your blog.

So as to do that, you have to do explore about their site. Peruse every one of the articles you can on their site. At that point make sense of if their perusers are propelled level, apprentices or transitional. Since that will have a major effect in the rush hour gridlock, you will create from your visitor post.

You would prefer not to compose a careful article on a learner's site. It will just make readers neglect your articles. Generally speaking ensure that you are obliging their gathering of people. Which means, you need to compose a fundamental article if their site is an essential site and the other way around.

Discover what is working

When you are doing your examination on the site, attempt to discover the most shared and the most seen post. That will enable you to make sense of what the group of onlookers needs. Attempt and compose a comparative post simply like the most prevalent one on their site. That will fulfill the site as they would get a great deal of perspectives and offers. Likewise, this will help you hugely support your blog subsequently developing your business.

Keep in mind, when you have the chance to compose on another person's blog, it isn't about you or your image. You are composing as a visitor, helping the site get more perspectives and offers. Visitor blogging will enable you to produce more traffic to your blog, however that ought not be your essential core interest.

In the event that you attempt and advance yourself in the visitor post, at that point odds of you landing more positions later on will be practically nothing. Trust me, you will get traffic from visitor posting yet don't advance yourself on the article. That being stated, I trust you have delighted in this book so far as we are arriving at its finish. The last two parts will tell you the best way to take your blog past the $10,000 a month point we have been discussing in this book.

By now you should have your product listing page built and your products on the way to the fulfillment center or waiting there ready to be sold! In this section I will be covering the most effective ways that you can start driving traffic to your product to make your initial sales. It's time to start making money!

Facebook and Instagram ads

Currently, both Facebook and Instagram are the most used social media platforms. This means that there is a great chance that your prospects are there. If properly done, you can generate traffic from there down to your website. You can convert the traffic to clients, who want to click more, watch your videos, and install your mobile apps.

Getting these results are possible, but you have to put efforts into it.

Facebook and Instagram Ads work together. You don't have to create an Instagram account before you can craft out an Instagram Ad. You can make use of your Facebook account. The option can be accessed in the settings of the account.

That's not all, as these social media channels permit you to reduce how much you spend on marketing, as your ads can easily be targeted to the right audience.

Let's say; you are promoting a dirt bike; you can easily have your Facebook and Instagram are targeted to those that are lovers of dirt bikes and their accessories.

One thing that a lot of marketers love about both ads is the fact that their targeting options are well defined. This means that you can choose whomever you want your product targeted to.

Instagram and Facebook are social networks, where people try to have fun, hence whatever you do there should be tailored to make their lives fun. No one will leave a fun activity to stare at a boring ad. A smart affiliate knows how to tailor their ads to capture the attention of their targeted audience.

Since Instagram and Facebook have a lot of targeting options, they allow businesses to reach their prospects by putting the ads on either the Instagram stories or news feed. This prevents the ads from coming off as being out of place.

Chapter 15 When to and not to use Amazon FBA?

Here is a story someone shared online

A guy, let's call him Jack, started selling on Amazon in 2017. He heard so many success stories to make his ears ache and he believed he could be part of the success story if he just opts-in without taking a second guess. How wrong he was.

We are all guilty of this – most of us or to be candid, all of us. We show the world what we are able to achieve, where our success can serve as an inspiration to others, where we can receive applause for what we have done, our hard work.

We keep the bad parts; no one wants to read a post titled 'my failure stories.' We write 'success stories.' And if possible, we exaggerate the good parts and hide information about the days where we thought we should rather quit and do something else.

Jack had just finished reading such a success story about Amazon FBA. He would make a lot of money, he thought.

He didn't have information about the program or how to go about it. So he started finding information online. He read books and blog post and all advice he could find on forums. Then he started.

According to the information he read, he sourced for products in China. They arrived. It was a popular niche, and soon his product was among a million others that are just similar yet not serving any other unique purpose than others. This was the beginning of his fall.

He sold little, made a meager profit. He tried to beat the competition as his mind had given him ideas. He thought about the possible ways to make his product rank better. He sat down, hoping his cost of sourcing for the products and the total investment of his time, knowledge and lessons would not go into waste. An idea came, a simple one, and it is what most people have done or are doing: he gave out some of his product for free in exchange for ranking and reviews.

In the end, it was a 'failure story.' He came out of it a better person but with an empty wallet and money that have gone into oblivion. If you catch him around and you ask for advice about Amazon FBA, he will offer the greatest and the most valuable lessons you may not find anywhere else.

Research is important

Research is important. If you have a person who is in the game already, they have valuable lessons to offer you. And guess what, it might cost nothing than sitting down and taking the advice seriously.

If there is no one you can run to, calm down, and read this chapter carefully. You might be running a risk of losing your money, depending on how much you invest for the first time.

On the brighter side, your first attempt could seem like you have hit the jackpot. You might decide to relax, cross your legs; Amazon is working hard, really hard to make you richer.

When not to use Amazon FBA

The best piece of advice is that you should try to verify the profitability of selling your product by employing a strategic process. You might try doing market research to know what people are actually buying. For instance, you can use an FBA calculator.

Moving on, here are other factors that indicate you shouldn't use the system. The risks are higher than the outcome.

1. You have a small number of items

You only have 40 pieces or less than that or the majority is on another platform, and they are selling fine. Then you should stick with that medium. Let others who have a higher number of items – in hundreds and thousands use FBA. The process of packaging items and moving it to Amazon warehouse coupled with Amazon charges and rules will not yield good returns with such a small number of items. The stress, return, and bureaucracy may not be worth it.

2. You have a small profit

It is good advice to do proper calculations if you want to sell on Amazon. Imagine you are selling a product with a small profit margin. If Amazon deducts sellers' fees and the cost of keeping your inventory with them, are you still making a profit?

This could mean you are not making a profit at all. So ensure you do your calculations. And you cannot increase your profit easily. There are competitions and price is one factor that can make a buyer scroll down to the next available seller. The topic about seller fees is one we will get to in this book.

3. Your product will attract more fees than average

Some products usually attract more fees than others, not because they are more valuable or expensive.

These are things you should note about your products

- Small
- Large
- Weighs a lot

Amazon will charge you more if your product is heavy or takes a lot of space. You should use the weight of your product to calculate the amount you will be charged as FBA fees then make a connection with your profit margin.

Your products are with another E-Commerce website with an older or outdated system of operation.

If you are selling on other newer platforms, it is easy for you to sell on Amazon. There is an easy automation process that allows you to sell using FBA if you are already using

- Shopify
- Big-Commerce

Older platforms are not easy to synchronize with FBA. And this could lower your chances of enjoying all the benefits of FBA.

When to use Amazon FBA

Once you have done an excellent job in determining the times you shouldn't be using Amazon FBA, it is time to do more than that and focus on when you should use the program. Again, you should be reminded that using the FBA calculator is a good decision which we will talk about later.

When to use FBA:

Your main sales platform is Amazon

If you have been using Amazon before, it will be good advice to join the FBA program. This will give you the opportunity to enjoy all the benefits of using Amazon's programs. For instance, you will be allowed into Amazon Prime, and there is the advertising, among other benefits.

Amazon will handle other tedious activities. These include:

- They will help you source for new products
- They will help improve your listings
- *It is their job to widen the customer base*

You have done your calculations

You can earn more and do less work when you have taken your time to calculate, and you have done adequate research. In this book, we will talk about the process of starting the Amazon FBA for success. With proper planning with the aid of the right information, you will be making a profit on the program.

You sell on other brands or subsidiaries of Amazon or channels that have a smooth relationship with Amazon

Selling on other platforms which are affiliated with Amazon is a huge boost for sales. FBA will enhance the multiple channel or network and help you reach a wider shipping network. Amazon has facilitated the program with what is called Multi-Channel Fulfillment (MCF). This allows you to sell and ship on third-party platforms while using a third party seller.

Tips for selling For New Amazon sellers

When you are new to something, you need guidance. You are in a new city, and there is no road sign, no poster to follow directions. Now a blind man is standing on the sidewalk with his little poodle. Would you ask him and expect directions to a place he has never seen before just that he has heard the sound of it?

That said, you need to be careful so as not to make mistakes. To that, here is some advice for beginners who want to make money selling on Amazon FBA.

Ignore the resources with outrageous ideas and success stories

You want to know what products people are buying on Amazon. You will find a lot of them, and many of them are already saturated. Many people will offer you the list of bestsellers on the platform for you to make your next billion. Follow it at your own risk. If you can't do something different from what the market is already offering, it is wise to move to something else.

The truth is that other people are looking for the same list of bestselling products, and you will end up on the same bus, overcrowded and fighting for fresh breath.

Weigh your options. Look at the market; make sure you stand a chance among the competitors before you dive in.

Follow trends only if you catch the train early

There is a new trend on Amazon; you find it today, check the number of sellers you see on the platform; they are just five or ten or just a little. You are early to the party, so take a sit and ask the waiter for your own dish. Start selling the product.

But if you are new to the game and you follow a trend which already has a hundred or more sellers, you are there to watch others killing it. Back out now before it's too late and your money is gone.

Keep an attentive eye on trends before there is a lot of noise on TV or social media. Those who make a lot of money by following trends are of two types, those who are lucky or those who have heard it early. You can be both.

Research like a drunk

Research everything and everything like a drunk. A drunk is a person who is not afraid to ask many questions, even the ones that seem stupid. But when you are reading and listening to the results of your research, you should put your ears down and dissect every piece of information like a toddler who has found a bewildering toy.

Another thing you must do is to understand the category which you want to sell. You might find out too late that there are restrictive barriers if you are selling in some categories. Also, you will want to research the approval processes before you start selling. We will get to it.

Sell only good stuff

So you have a product, or you have outsourced a product, but you don't know if it is of good quality. You didn't use it yourself to determine if it is worth the money. Once you buyers find out you are selling a piece of worthless product, you are on your way to lose sales and with a lot of bad reviews. This could be the end of sales on Amazon. People rarely give a review on Amazon so ensure you are getting the good ones to avoid doom.

For starters, you should have firsthand experience with a product to verify its functionality, quality, and durability. Check other sellers and see what people are saying about the products. Now you can address the issues or simply change the product if you think there is no chance to make a difference.

Source cheaper products

You need to do some calculations before you jump into the sales of a particular product. This will also help to ensure you will beat the competition with a lower price than others. On Amazon, price is an essential factor that can influence sales.

Before you decide to sell at a price, you need to calculate all the charges Amazon is taking to ensure you are making a profit with your sales. You will want to calculate the cost of shipping, sourcing, Amazon fees, and promotions you have made, and you will want to use that in determining the selling price of your product.

With such additional costs, your price might seem higher. And if you are selling an expensive item, people will run for cheaper competitors. So before you sell, check the prices that other sellers have set for their products and aim to beat them.

Don't forget the previous point anyway.

Sell products you are passionate about wisely

Although selling a product you are passionate about can bring a kind of joy, you should try to analyze the decisions you are making. When it comes to such products, sellers are likely to get emotional. They wonder why the sale is not moving in accordance with the level of passion they have. Well, buyers do not share the same passion, and you need to give them what they want to buy if you want to make sales. You need to be always logical about sales, not emotional.

Check if the product is patented

Selling a product that is patented is illegal. So if you are a private label seller, you must check if the product you are getting from a wholesaler is patented or not. This is something you must examine closely because the wholesaler will not tell you. Selling a patented product can qualify you for a lawsuit.

Do a lot of work on your product listings

Private label sellers are the ones that do their product listings. You are required to set up your listing and make it stand out. Start with finding a good product, you should always be on the lookout for the best products out there. Next, you will put that same effort in creating a listing that is irresistible for your buyers. Of course, it requires a lot of work. But then you have to remember you are not the only seller on the platform, and people will not know your product unless your listing is doing a good advertisement and conversion. So what will you do?

Write a good copy on your listing, using keywords creatively. With this done, you will improve the chances of your product being found, and you will persuade buyers to make a purchase with effective copy. If you can't write one, perhaps you should hire a copywriter.

Another important thing is the quality of images you put up there. You don't want to use a photograph taken with your smartphone and expect to stand out from the competition. You need to invest in professional photography. You can find affordable ones around you.

Stick to the rules

You will find out some sellers on Amazon are breaking some of the policies of the platform. They call it the 'black hat' techniques. They will increase sales by generating more reviews. They manipulate the process of reviewing a product. Some of them will get away with it, and you might be lucky or unlucky. Amazon will come down on you like a heavy rock if they find out you are playing games with their policies. They have intensified their strategies on finding out sellers who are engaging in review frauds.

You must improve your listing

If you are making sales, you might think your listing does not need readjustment. This is the first mistake most beginners make. Things can change over time; the keywords people use in their search might change over time. You have to monitor your listing and how it is driving results, especially if you are not making sales as expected.

Many private label sellers also make the same mistake, but you should not afford to. You should check other competitor's listing and see how they are done. Find new keywords your buyers are using and ensure you are up to date in the business. You can also ask a trusted friend to check your listing on your behalf and give you feedback.

Put your product in the right category

You might think your product has a better chance if you put it in a different category. Of course, you might earn the bestseller badge you are craving for, but you are missing out on some buyers. Why? Some buyers will go to a subcategory to search for a particular product, and if they can't find yours, they will go for the available option.

Chapter 16 Tips for Success

Free inventory from your house: In my house, and likely yours as well, there are those items that you have not been used, ever! Not since you bought it because it was on sale, or there was a discount on the commodity. You could have used it once and return to the furthest corner of your closet or kitchen cabinet; no matter the case, these items can be turned into cash or better, profit! All you have to do is ship them to Amazon for that to happen.

Go hunting! Look through your book shelves, not all books in your library you like them, get them out and create space for the series you have been dying to read in your house and also reduce clutter. Go into your cabinets in your kitchen, your kids (if you have any) rooms with their permission, of course, your room as well and get rid of anything that you do not use at all. Some items you can get will surprise you; as these items can be used to create profits on Amazon.

Take the initiative and involve your family, friends, and neighbor-if they are willing to do so-and use all these items to earn cash! It can be an excellent way to spend a weekend, go through your trash to make money.

Using dunnage for shipments: The stuff, either puffy or protective wrapper, which you use to wrap your load to protect them from touching the sides of your shipping box that is the definition of dunnage.

There are various things you can use to protect your items so that they can arrive safely to your customer without breakage. The commodities in the list below are things you are most likely going to have in your house already. You can use:

- A newspaper blanket

- A variety of small cardboard boxes for glass items

- From your online arbitrage purchases, you can use the air pillows in them

- Tie printed papers in your everyday plastic grocery bags. This is to protect your shipment from getting in contact with the newsprint.

Free boxes from grocery stores for shipment: At the beginning of your Amazon FBA business, there won't be the need for you to pay for delivery boxes as you might not have the cash for it or you want to save the money you have for something else. You can get shipping boxes for free from grocery stores, your neighbors who have moved recently, or your friends or colleagues that have moved as well as places that recycle their old boxes. This will save you tons of cash. Make sure you select the best boxes out of all those that are at your disposal.

From the grocery store, ask the employees or attendees when they are restocking their shelves if you can have some of the boxes they are using. They are likely to let you come and collect to your heart's content or even when they are restocking come and get the boxes from their aisles.

Lighter fluid to remove price stickers: When reusing shipment boxes, there is the likelihood of price stickers being on them. Removing them is one struggle you will have to endure if you are trying to save money, but getting rid of the sticker residue is another struggle all on its own. When it comes to dealing with the residue from price stickers lighter fluid will do the trick every time.

Be careful when handling the liquid, and this will guarantee the removal of the residue. The process is quite simple, and all you will require is a Scotty peeler to remove the labels. You can use a Ronsonol lighter fluid. To do this, you will:

- Pour some of the lighter fluid on the sticker residue you want to get rid off

- Wait for a few minutes, approximately 5 minutes before you can try and remove the labels

- Using your Scotty peeler, gently try and pry the tag off.

Free inventory from Freecycle.org: Join a group of your area on Freecycle Network to be able to see what people are getting rid of or giving away for free that you can use for your shipments. You might be shocked by the number of things that you can source using this network. I got board games- both used and new-; books, in boxes; kitchen appliances, among other things.

The way it works is:

- Claim an item on the Freecycle Network

- The owner will leave it on the front porch or sidewalk

- Go and collect your item!

And that's it! Fairly easy and straightforward. This makes it easy for you to coordinate with the owner as you will get to set a time that you will pass by to collect it.

Boxes from arbitrage purchases: To be honest, most of the sourcing that you do for this type of business is through online sourcing. This means that there will be shipments sent to you in boxes. Thus you can use these same boxes for your shipments to Amazon. But you have to go to be careful and remove all bar codes. This can be removed or covered up before you can use the UPS label or Amazon.

Productivity tools: There are times when you just need to have a nap without worrying over unnecessarily about the way your online store is doing or how the shipments are fairing or remember if you sent a reply to your customer's comment. Below are some productivity tools that can help you shave off some of that time:

- IFTTT (If This Then That): This is mainly used by sellers on Amazon or eBay. The app is used to alert the sellers of when sales have been made, or stock has been added back into inventory, or it has been added elsewhere.

- Facebook News Eradicator: With various sellers mainly spending their time on this social media platform going through the different FBA groups, it can take much of your time without you realizing it. To help you with this, this eradicator cuts down your extension extremely low. It allows you not to spend so much time on the internet getting to know what all your sources on Amazon

FBA are talking about or all seller community groups.

- Cleer Pro: is an online app for online arbitrage. It is a software that makes it easier for you as a vendor to browse easily when trying to look for deals, items or doing your research on Amazon.com

- Gmail Canned Responses: typing a similar response over and over again can get exhausting, and no one wants that kind of stress. Therefore, this app allows you to formulate a response that is going to reply automatically to the type of replies that come from your customers. The same app can be used to respond to an email you get in your Amazon seller inbox. Since Amazon allows you to use your email to respond to customers instead of creating a particular kind of email address, you can use this app.

- Flashback Express: it can only be used on Windows, unfortunately. It can be used to quickly capture and annotate your voice and then upload the video on your screen. This can be used to communicate something that is in your store. Or deliver something that is on your screen to a colleague or your occasional customer. This makes the message more personal than ever, and it can be the best way to explain something to your customers in an easier manner, and it can make you quite popular among other clients. It can bring you more customers as well.

- Unroll.me: There are dozens upon dozens of emails that you receive from a seller on a daily basis about different offers that you are going to get from Amazon. The difference between having this app and not having it, is you are required to need to keep clicking delete or unsubscribe manually. This app allows you to unsubscribe from those emails or offers that you do not want to have in bulk. There are tutorials online that you can use to help you navigate through the app with ease.

Time saving hacks: To save your time as a salesperson when screening your items and scanning them, you can use the $0.00 buy cost to help you when browsing for items mainly in the app's field "Buy$." The time that you spend typing at the expense of the item is deducted since it costs nothing! You can use a calculator to subtract the actual buying price of the item from the profit price and decide on whether you will purchase the item or you will forgo it.

At times, it is not necessary for you to do the math of whether you will get to buy the product; all you have got to do is check if the price you are buying the item is higher or lower than the price of the profit you are bound to make.

An example would be if the cost of the head gear is at $12.99 and the profit you are required to make is at $9.99; you will not buy the item since it costs more than what you are going to get from the profit.

Other ways of reducing the scanning process are through downloading the Amazon 1Button app. It is an extension from chrome that shows you the price of the item you require, and it does the searching or looking or scanning for you.

An instance would be when looking for game boards; the app will let you know if the game is sold on Amazon and the price of the game. This saves you the trouble of going through Amazon trying to find the game and if it is even available and the price as well.

Keep in mind that not always does the search engine provide the results that you are looking for and at times the items might not even be available or found.

Make sure you invest in the best supplies you possibly can get your hands on. There are the common denominators of supplies that most Amazon sellers have in their arsenal and use them. Most of them swear by these items and can attest to their immense help when carrying out their daily sales.

Have a business credit card and checking account: in your daily life, you have a personal credit card that you use mainly to buy your items and spend it as you wish. You also, most definitely (if not, get one ASAP!) keep track of your expenses and savings as well.

You can have a software tracking app on your every expense charged to your credit card, be it personal or business. For the Amazon FBA, you need to have a business credit card and checking account to keep track of what you are spending on and where your money goes. This card and account need to be different from your credit and checking account.

You can use Quickbooks as a way to keep track of your personal and business accounts and credit cards. The app allows you to:

- Keep track of what you have spent
- Know how much you owe your credit card and
- Where you shop at

Run your business like a business: **With this being your business, even if you are running it at your house, you need to run it like one. To make shipping easier, create your shipping and prepping station.**

It doesn't have to be anything fancy or too elaborate, get a small table and lean it against a wall. Have drawers (they could be colored or whatever pattern you prefer) close by that house all your poly bags, shipping tapes, scissors, liquid fluid and any other necessary appliance that you need to wrap your shipping items and put them in your box.

Having or creating order in your house can help you run your business very smoothly. The station will help you reduce the time spent running around looking for scissors, the shipping tape or trying to figure out where to lay your merchandise at so that you can work.

The area around your working station can function as your prepping station, where you gather all your necessary items, put them together before you move to your working station to put the final touches on your product before shipping them off to your customer.

The station can act as a studio of some sort. When you have laid out your items on the table, you can take a picture of the items and use them for your store on Amazon. The pictures can be edited; changing the color in the background to pure white t put it on the product listing images section of your site.

Know a good deal when you see one: While finding a niche is important to the long term strength of your FBA store, the most important rule of FBA is that if you can make a profit on it then you should sell it. As such, regardless of what the product is if you find yourself staring at a sale that is 75 percent off or more then there is always going to be room enough there for you to make a profit on the item. The key to not putting too much work into this type of passive income is to always passively be on the lookout for good deals and be ready and able to jump on them when you see them because the best deals are never going to stick around for very long.

Care about your seller rating: Just because you letting Amazon do most of the heavy lifting doesn't mean that you can let your store run on autopilot. Specifically, you are going to want to be aware of your seller rating and do everything you can to keep it as high as possible. If you sell faulty merchandise or items that fall apart quickly then this number will drop rapidly which means you will want to consider all the costs of a particular product, not just what you pay to take direct ownership of the product. What's more, if you make a habit of selling unreliable items then Amazon can drop you from the service for hurting their image, something that you will obviously want to avoid at all costs.

Consider each purchase carefully: The best online retail arbitrage products are those that are heavily discounted, irrespective of the type of product in question. As a general rule, if you find anything, literally anything that is marked down 75 percent from its original price, then you can likely find a way to sell it for a profit online; whether it is worth it is another question. Another great choice are items that you can purchase in bulk cheaply now, before waiting for natural scarcity to set in six months or so down the line when your investment will pay off in spades.

A great example of this are toys you can purchase from a dollar store that are based on properties that are never going to go out of style such as Disney properties like Princesses, Star Wars or Marvel superheroes. Many of these products are only ever sold at dollar stores which means that after the initial stock dries up there will be thousands of parents out there looking for character specific merchandise that their child has not consumed yet. If you aren't interested in waiting, you can instead group a number of themed items together, knock a fraction of the total profit off and sell the total as a true bargain.

For example, if you purchase five Disney Princess puzzles for a total of $5, knowing that each typically sells for $5 on Amazon, then you can sell all five for $20, still have the group seen as the value, and even make more than a 50 percent profit on the transaction. If you pursue this course of action, you are going to generate a unique UPC code for the group of products, though you can use the same UPC code for multiple groups if applicable.

Don't forget about social media: The most essential social media for any company or brand to have is Facebook. Pretty much everybody uses Facebook, and having an active Facebook page is absolutely essential. Do whatever you can in order to build your Facebook fan base. Your posts aren't always going to get a ton of traction, but any traction and any traffic matters... plus, if you make a really good post, you're going to see a lot of traffic come from it naturally. That's just how it works with social media.

You're also going to want to consider getting Twitter and Instagram. These aren't quite as popular as Facebook and are more geared towards people in the 16 to 30 crowd, so if your niche aims at people who are older, then you may not have as much success on these. However, having a popular following on these networks can make a lot of difference for you as a company if you follow through with it appropriately and make a lot of posts.

Finally, you're going to want to set up a Snapchat. Snapchat is potentially one of the best marketing platforms because unlike other forms of social media, where only a portion of your followers can see your content without specifically going to your page, a story on Snapchat is visible to all of your followers. If you have a particularly visually appealing niche, Snapchat can be a great way to show people what you're up to and what's up next on your blog. This extra traffic and these return users will, in turn, lead to a big return on your affiliate marketing products.

Conclusion

Working with Amazon is like working with millions of sellers at the same time. Given the restricted categories of sales with Amazon, you will find a swarm of sellers selling the same commodities like you do. You will get to know about many more such things when you start working with Amazon FBA program of the company.

Being persistent with selling is the key to make success in this field. Like many other careers, Amazon FBA requires you to be determined and find ways to make maximum profit. But, you must have figured out that it is not very complicated as it seemed to you earlier. You just need to spare a few hours every day or every week and stick to your routine.

Make the most out of Amazon FBA once you have signed up for it. You already know that you do not need to spend a fortune to start with this program. You can start with a manageable amount that you can afford and then increase your investment. It might take time but, in the end,, you will have a successful part time business in hand, yielding you good money.

You will find many examples of people, who had started with Amazon FBA as a part time business, but now they have become the experts of its statistics and have adopted it full time. We would not recommend that you quit everything and start dreaming of becoming wealthy with Amazon FBA. Give it a few hours in a week and then think about working on it full time if you can sustain with investments.

Now that you know the basics of Amazon FBA, go ahead with beginning the program and explore it inside out. Make the most of Seller Central and your Seller account and no one can stop you from making a fortune with Amazon!

www.ingramcontent.com/pod-product-compliance
Lightning Source LLC
Chambersburg PA
CBHW070619220526
45466CB00001B/57